Eli

COUNTRY COOKING

Elisabeth Luard's
COUNTRY COOKING

EBURY PRESS
London

NOTE This book was previously published under the title: *Country Living A Taste of the Country.*

Author biography

Elisabeth Luard has written many previous books, including *European Peasant Cookery*, *European Festival Food* and *The Flavours of Andalucía*, for which she received a Glenfiddich award in 1992. She writes a weekly column for the *Scotsman* and her first novel, *Emerald*, was published in 1994. She divides her time between Wales and the island of Mull off the Scottish coast.

First published 1993

This edition published in 1996 by Ebury Press,
Random House, 20 Vauxhall Bridge Road, London SW1V 2SA

3 5 7 9 10 8 6 4 2

Text copyright © Elisabeth Luard 1993

Random House Australia (Pty) Limited
20 Alfred Street, Milsons Point, Sydney
New South Wales 2061, Australia

Random House New Zealand Limited
18 Poland Road, Glenfield
Auckland 10, New Zealand

Random House South Africa (Pty) Limited
PO BOX 337, Bergvlei, South Africa

Random House UK Limited Reg. No. 954009

A CIP catalogue record for this book is available from the British Library.

ISBN: 0 09 181270 4

Designed by the Senate and Bob Vickers

Printed and bound in Great Britain by Mackays of Chatham plc, Kent

CONTENTS

The strength of country cooking has always # Introduction
lain in good ingredients perfectly and simply
prepared. When, some years ago, *Country Living* magazine asked me to
find out if the traditions of rural cookery were still alive and well, I was
happy to embark on the search. With photographer and wild-food expert
Roger Phillips (or sometimes Jacqui Hurst) and *Country Living*'s editor
Francine Lawrence, we managed to poke our noses into rural cooking pots
all over these islands and further afield. It was a real delight to find tried-
and-true family recipes still being prepared, often with the help of modern
labour-saving devices, but with a fine appreciation of seasonal ingredients
and a respect for traditional skills. Our travels taught me that we remain
remarkably local in our culinary habits and you can see the evidence in
the recipes in this book, whether traditional favourites or new ways with
familiar home-grown ingredients.

Traditionally, rural recipes are dictated by landscape, seasonality,
availability of fuel and access to long-established trade-routes; ingredients
are naturally limited by that which can be harvested, husbanded or
gathered locally. Yet we have seen many changes since the days when
isolated rural communities had little access to imported goods. At the
beginning of modern times, the new-world vegetables – potatoes, tomatoes, maize, beans, marrows, peppers – dramatically changed the old
world's eating habits. Refrigeration and efficient transport systems now
ensure year-round supplies of fresh food to town and country dweller alike.

The human factor cannot be discounted in determining what makes up
good regional cooking. There are exceptional cooks, natural innovators,
who adapt and refine techniques, add new flavourings and import new
ideas to improve existing recipes. Immigration and emigration bring in new
skills and flavours: Britain owes many of its storecupboard relishes to the
Raj, many of its fish dishes to the sailors who pass through its ports.

Nevertheless, the quality of the raw materials dictates the excellence of
the dish. In cookery as with Greta Garbo's beauty, it's the bone structure
that counts. Ingredients can be as cheap and simple as you please – which

often means home-grown and in season – as long as they are the best and the freshest of their kind.

I have cooked for my family – husband and four growing children – in kitchens all over Europe, from the Pillars of Hercules to the Hebrides, and the only kitchen instrument I consider indispensable (even more important than haute-cuisine's razor sharp knives) is a large kitchen table. The three-yard-long scrubbed boards, now happily installed in my Welsh kitchen, accompanied us whenever possible on our travels. The table was made for me in the workshop of a Spanish shipwright who repaired the sturdy wooden fishing boats which patrol the Pillars of Hercules. On it I can spread out and admire the fruits of the day's marketing – an essential prelude to deciding what to do with the ingredients. In the Hebrides, the morning's haul might put me in mind of a dish of perfect floury potatoes (they grow best in the damp peaty soil of the Western Isles), cooked in their skins and mashed with fine-sliced leeks and milk, with a knob of butter to melt into a pool of creamy sauce. A morning in one of the fishing ports of the Sussex coast might yield a haul of queen scallops, most delicate of shellfish, to be baked briefly in their shells and served with lemon and buttered bread. Any winter market will produce fine, sweet root vegetables for a slow-cooked lamb stew, leeks for a creamy soup, turnips and swedes for a delicate purée to be served with the best butcher's sausages.

None of my earlier life, nor a pre-marriage year spent learning the catering trade at the Eastbourne School of Domestic Economy, prepared me for the demands of life as I found it in the early 1960s in one of the last rural peasant communities left in western Europe. While my London-born children were still young, circumstance installed us all in a remote forested valley in Andalucía in southern Spain. The peasant farmers and goatherds who tended the stony meadows and olive groves watered by the little Guadelmesi river had no access to supermarkets or freezer-food stores. Lentils and chickpeas for their soups and stews had to be sown, watered, harvested and dried. Eggs had to be fetched from beneath the warm breast feathers of an irritable, sharp-beaked hen. Wheat was threshed by a donkey pulling a sled whose design was known to Stone Age man, and then taken to be ground in a mill whose vaulted barrel roof had been built by the Moors, driven from Spain by Ferdinand and Isabella in the same year that Columbus set out on his great adventure. The bread itself was baked in a wood-fired whitewashed oven built of brick and adobe, and each loaf was pricked by hand with the baker's initials.

The children were at home immediately. My neighbours, as is usual in isolated rural communities, took my small, ignorant foreign children into their special care. Space was found for them in the little local school and they were soon acquiring skills regarded as rather more essential than the alphabet: how to make and set a rabbit trap, which particular rock pools to trawl for freshwater crayfish, how to hobble and harness a donkey. They were let into the secrets of where the sweetest figs grew in an abandoned orchard, which hedgerow plants to nibble on the way home from school, and which could be collected to flavour a stew. On their expeditions up the oleander-lined streams they discovered where mushrooms grew in autumn, and where the wild asparagus sprouted in the burnt black earth which marked the path of a summer brush-fire.

Meanwhile, my neighbours took it upon themselves to tutor me in those skills in which my mother had clearly neglected to instruct me. We kept, slaughtered and salted down our own pig for the winter larder. We grew our own garlic and onions and plaited them into skeins for store. Milk still warm from the cow was delivered daily from across the valley by a young man who measured the rich creamy liquid into a jug from a donkey-borne churn. The Christmas goose, fattened on the valley's acorns, arrived on foot. Our cheese came from a neighbouring goatherd. Honey came from someone's cousin's bees, pastured on the rosemary and thyme which covered the hills behind us. From the lip of the valley on a clear day we could see across the Straits of Gibraltar to the mountains of Africa, and spices bought from the market spice-lady gave an eastern flavour to local dishes.

When we all moved to Languedoc for the children to have a year's schooling in French, our new neighbours there performed the same service of instruction. Our meals were dictated by the changing year and I learnt the correct way to layer a cassoulet, the cuts of beef which went into a pot-au-feu, which fish were indispensable for a bouillabaisse.

Such seasonal and regional pleasures are available to us all, whatever country we live in. The more we insist on quality, the more available it becomes as our suppliers discover there is a market for their best produce. Sometimes your butcher, fishmonger or greengrocer may need some coaxing, or you may have to go further afield and spend a little more to buy good home-grown ingredients – but you will not then have to spend money and time to disguise shortcomings in the raw materials.

The best available ingredients, in the hands of a cook who loves good food, are all that is needed if we are to eat as well as recipes promise or memory serves.

*In the days before
we all had access
to imported fresh
vegetables, wild*

SPRING

greens were the first welcome signs of spring, doubly valued after the long winter when stores of root vegetables were almost exhausted. Children who walked to school enjoyed the clean flavours of young leaves picked from the hedgerow – hawthorn and hazel, beech and tender asparagus-flavoured hop shoots.

Every gardener would leave a patch of nettles so that the first leaves could be used in spring soups. The nettles provided a nursery-patch for butterfly larvae, too, rewarding good husbandry with a flight of bright-winged tortoiseshells and blazing peacocks to dance in the summer meadows.

Our wild larder is still there for the gathering – and innovative cooks such as Patricia Hegarty at Hope End in Herefordshire make good use of the young leaves others might consider weeds. Her favourites include acid-sharp sorrel and the bitter-clean flavour of tansy, and she uses the powerful pungent fronds of lovage to perfume tiny soufflés.

The first week of March traditionally saw the opening of the fishing ports. With the winter storms abated, the inshore fleet can once more venture into the fishing grounds. Our island-nation has always made good use of its sea-harvest, most prolific of wild resources, and the need to conserve stocks is recognised by the fishermen themselves.

Ocean-husbandry and fish-farming, although still in their infancy, seem set to become the agri-business of the future. Shellfish farming has been established round the shores of Britain for well over a thousand years. The beds of Colchester and Whitstable were cropped *in Roman times, and, until the introduction of modern fishing-nets, rope-farmed mussels were used not only as a delectable dish for humans, but to bait the herring-lines. Although salmon-farming remains a highly contentious issue with those concerned about environmental pollution, important lessons have been learned, and the industry has brought back the noble fish, once the food of the poor, within reach of most pockets.*

The sea served (and still serves) not only as a food-source, but also as a highway. Transport has always been the lifeblood of isolated communities – bringing in not only those necessities which cannot be grown, gathered or husbanded locally, but also luxuries. Mail-order provides the modern answer to rural isolation, both for the suppliers and the supplied. Anne Grimsdale describes the outer ring of the M25 motorway as a gastronomic desert – so she simply reaches for the telephone to have the best of everything, from organic meat to fresh oysters, delivered from all over the country.

In the Garden of England, livestock fattened on the rich salt pastures of Kent's Romney Marshes provide the finest meat – and there's no better authority than a butcher's wife when it comes to roasting a crown of spring lamb, or stewing well-matured beef with locally-brewed ale.

Whether home-gathered, sea-harvested or postman-delivered, the spring is the time to look for the best and freshest of the new season's ingredients.

Patricia Hegarty is that rare and

Spring in Herefordshire

endangered breed: a truly regional cook. Even better, her skills are available to the rest of us: Patricia and her husband John run a hotel and restaurant, the much-praised Hope End, a romantic, minareted country house sheltering in the rolling foothills of the Malverns. Patricia was born and bred in Herefordshire, and her family has lived there for 600 years; 20 generations rooted in the rich earth of old England have bred a strong sense of the value of such permanence and the responsibilities it brings. Cathedral builders know the value of planting oaks.

'It's comforting to know people have performed the same rural tasks for so many centuries before – it gives you a sense of timelessness. My family comes from Colwall just near here, and my immediate ancestors were in the provision trade. They were fruit-growers and farmers, and had preserve-making and canning businesses. They made cider vinegar, which was used in enormous quantities for preserving food before refrigeration. So we've been in the provisioning business for a long time.'

It's 15 years since the Hegartys welcomed their first customers and Patricia has not only built up an international reputation for fine cooking, but has done so the hard way: by keeping a thoroughly English table. The English tradition is unforgiving: its excellence depends on the best of native-grown ingredients prepared with skill and innocence. In the kitchen at Hope End a rack of spring lamb from a Ledbury butcher, who slaughters and hangs his own meat, needs no sauce but its own juices, perfumed with rosemary from the flowerpot by the kitchen door. A delicate rhubarb jelly is sweetened with honey from the bees that pollinate the cider orchards surrounding the house.

'You have to remember that because English cooking is so simple the raw materials must be perfect,' stresses Patricia. 'That means growing or selecting them all yourself; then there's nothing to beat traditional English cooking. We are fortunate to have the garden, and good suppliers for meat, poultry and fish.'

Without a doubt it is the produce of John's magnificent potager, brought straight from the garden to the kitchen door, that underpins Patricia's fine cooking. Very good soil and 15 years of organic farming have produced 200 varieties of fruit and vegetables, with new ones constantly being added and less successful experiments dropped. There is a nut grove and all the soft fruit the English summer can ripen. But it is the vegetables that are the true glory of the beautiful walled garden: cardoon and sea kale, salsify and scorzonera, turnip-rooted parsley and crisp-leaved lettuce. The neatly hoed beds slope down from a greenhouse full of ripening tomatoes, aubergines, peppers and flourishing vines.

Patricia wanders down the rows of vegetables, planning her menus at source. 'There's no doubt,' she says, surveying her fertile valley, 'that here we have the very best of England.'

Sorrel Soup

Our ancestors welcomed the appearance of the first blood-cleansing green herbs: young nettles (pick the top four leaves only, and be sure to wear gloves) make a clean-tasting iron-rich broth; young dandelion leaves are still appreciated all over Europe as a salad.

Serves 6

50 g (2 oz) unsalted butter
1 small onion, skinned and
  chopped
1 small potato, peeled and thinly
  sliced
18 young sorrel leaves
1.1 litres (2 pints) hot chicken stock
  or water

sea salt
black pepper
2 egg yolks to thicken (optional)

To serve
garlic croûtons

Melt the butter in a large saucepan over a moderate heat and stir in the onion. Cook until softened, then add the potato to absorb the butter and continue cooking for a moment.

Wash the sorrel leaves, removing and discarding any thick red stems which may be bitter. Tear the leaves into pieces and stir them in the buttery mixture until they wilt. Add the stock or water; bring to the boil and simmer for 15 minutes. If you prefer a sharper flavour and brighter colour, add the sorrel at the end of the cooking time. Remove from the heat and let the soup cool for a moment.

Purée the mixture in a blender and then sieve it back into the pan. Reheat gently; season with salt and pepper. For a richer, more velvety broth, stir a ladleful of the hot soup into the beaten egg yolks and then whisk back into the mixture. Reheat the soup gently, but don't let it boil. Serve with crisp garlic croûtons.

Little Lovage Soufflés

Lovage is perfect in a soufflé, which needs a strong flavour to permeate the frothy eggs.

Serves 8 as a starter

40 g (1½ oz) unsalted butter
75 g (3 oz) wholemeal breadcrumbs
bunch of fresh lovage leaves, to taste
25 g (1 oz) wholemeal flour
300 ml (½ pint) fresh milk

5 large free-range eggs, separated
30 ml (2 tbsp) finely grated fresh Parmesan cheese
sea salt
black pepper

Butter 8 individual ramekins with 15 g (½ oz) of the butter. Sprinkle with half the breadcrumbs to prevent the soufflés from sticking as they rise. Reserve remaining crumbs.

Melt the rest of the butter in a small saucepan over a low heat. Stir in the lovage leaves. When they have wilted, stir in the flour and cook for 1 minute. Gradually add the milk to make a sauce. Remove from the heat and process the mixture in a food processor until the sauce is spotted with green. Let it cool and then incorporate the egg yolks, half the Parmesan cheese and a generous seasoning of salt and pepper. The mixture should be fairly runny.

Whisk the egg whites until they are stiff. Fold them carefully into the soufflé with a metal spoon. Fill the prepared ramekins. Mix the remaining breadcrumbs and Parmesan cheese together and sprinkle over the tops.

Bake in the oven at 220°C (425°F) mark 7 for 10 minutes, or until they are nicely risen and still slightly moist in the middle. Serve immediately.

Variation   To make one large soufflé that will serve 4 as a main course, butter-and-breadcrumb a 15 cm (6 inch) soufflé dish. Fill with the lovage mixture and top with breadcrumbs and Parmesan. Bake at 200°C (400°F) mark 6 for 35–40 minutes.

LOVAGE

Lovage crowns are among the first to put out shoots in the spring garden. Lovage is a powerfully aromatic herb – something like unblanched celery with a touch of anise – and a little goes a long way.

Lamb Noisettes in Perry Sauce

Perry, fermented pear juice from the old Herefordshire varieties like Barland and Moorcroft, makes a sauce for tender lamb, perfumed with the first shoots of rosemary.

Serves 6

12–18 lamb cutlets, depending on size
black pepper
1 small onion, skinned and chopped
1 small carrot, chopped
1 celery stalk, sliced
1 bay leaf
fresh English parsley

25 g (1 oz) wholemeal flour
300 ml (½ pint) medium-dry perry
sea salt

To finish
rosemary sprigs
medlar or redcurrant jelly

Bone the cutlets but save everything. Remove the eye of the meat and carefully pare away most of the fat along the length of the cutlet until you are left with a thin strip of skin. Wrap this round the eye of the meat and secure with a cocktail stick. Season with freshly ground pepper.

Make the stock: put all the bones and trimmings, including the fat, in a roasting tin with the onion, carrot and celery, and roast in the oven at 200°C (400°F) mark 6 for about 45 minutes, or until the bones and vegetables are well browned.

Remove and strain off the fat. Reserve the fat and tip the roasted bones and vegetables into a saucepan; add the bay leaf and parsley and enough water to cover. Bring to the boil; reduce the heat and leave to simmer for 30 minutes. You will need about 300 ml (½ pint) of stock for the sauce, so strain it, then let it reduce further.

Make the sauce: melt 15 ml (1 tbsp) of the reserved lamb fat in a saucepan; stir in the flour and let it cook for a minute. Stir in the perry vigorously, plus any meat jelly that has accumulated beneath the lamb fat. Let it all bubble up, then whisk in the lamb stock. Bring to the boil and simmer for about 5 minutes, whisking to keep the sauce smooth. Taste and season.

Grill the lamb noisettes under a medium high grill for about 12 minutes, turning them three times. When they are done, transfer them to a warm dish and remove the cocktail sticks. Mix any meat juices from the grill pan into the sauce and strain through a fine sieve into a warm gravy boat or jug.

Serve each portion garnished with a sprig of rosemary and a spoonful of medlar or redcurrant jelly.

Rhubarb and Honey Jelly

Make this delicate coral-pink jelly with the first stalks of rhubarb from the forcing pot.

Serves 6

900 g (2 lb) fresh rhubarb
45 ml (3 tbsp) honey (or to taste)
6 leaves gelatine

To finish
whipped cream
toasted flaked almonds

Cut the rhubarb into short lengths, discarding the green and white parts of the stalk. Put it in a heavy saucepan with 30 ml (2 tbsp) water; cover and cook for about 30 minutes until very soft and juicy. Strain off the juice into a measuring jug: you will need 900 ml (1½ pints). Stir the honey into the hot juice and leave it to dissolve.

Meanwhile, cover the gelatine leaves with a splash of cold water in a shallow dish and put them aside to soften. When the rhubarb juice has cooled to finger-temperature, carefully stir in the gelatine leaves one by one, making sure they all mix in. Strain into a glass bowl or individual wine glasses. Chill in the refrigerator for about 4 hours, or until set.

To serve, top with whipped cream and almond flakes.

Chestnut and Pear Flan

The secret of feather-light wholemeal pastry is to roll it out very thinly.

Serves 6

For the wholemeal pastry
50 g (2 oz) wholemeal flour
25 g (1 oz) cold unsalted butter
5 ml (1 tsp) ground roasted nuts
    (optional)
5–10 ml (1–2 tsp) icing sugar or
    finely ground demerara sugar
    (optional)
30 ml (2 tbsp) ice-cold water

For the filling
100 g (4 oz) dried chestnuts, soaked
    overnight
3–4 large dessert pears
450 ml (³/4 pint) dry perry
1 small piece vanilla pod
45 ml (3 tbsp) honey

To glaze
redcurrant or medlar jelly

Make the pastry in a food processor. Sift the flour into the bowl and chop up the butter, which must be used straight from the refrigerator. Mix at slow speed until it resembles fine breadcrumbs. Add the nuts, if using, and sugar. Turn the speed up a notch and add the iced water. Watch until the pastry gathers itself up in a ball, then turn the motor off immediately. Allow the pastry to rest for at least 20 minutes.

Roll it out as thinly as possible on a cold floured surface and use to line a tart tin. Line the pastry with greaseproof paper and weigh it down with dried beans. Make sure the beans go right into the corners. Bake in the oven at 200°C (400°F) mark 6 for 10 minutes. Remove the beans and paper, prick the base of the pastry and bake for a further 5 minutes.

Peel, halve and core the pears. Put them in a saucepan with the perry and poach for about 15 minutes until lightly cooked. (Timing will depend on the ripeness of the pears.) When they are done, lift them out and allow to cool.

Drain the chestnuts and simmer in the pear-poaching liquid with the piece of vanilla pod until tender. This could take up to 2 hours if the chestnuts are very hard. Top up with water if necessary. When the chestnuts are cooked, remove the vanilla pod and process the chestnuts with the honey and enough of the cooking liquid to produce a smooth purée.

Spread the chestnut purée over the pastry base and arrange the poached pears on top, cut-side down. Melt the red fruit jelly in a bowl over a pan of hot water and use to glaze the pears. Serve the flan with thick Jersey cream.

CHESTNUT AND PEAR FLAN

In the autumn Patricia Hegarty makes this lovely dessert with chestnuts from the 300-year-old trees in the park, and uses any hard little pears which have not ripened on the trees in the orchard.

Tansy Custard

Tansy is one of the Elizabethan strewing herbs, used to keep floors sweet-scented and fly-free. A member of the daisy family, it has an odd, slightly bitter, chrysanthemum flavour. Thyme or rosemary can be used instead, but tansy gives the real flavour of Tudor England.

Serves 6

225 g (8 oz) well-rinsed spinach (for colour)
about 12 tansy leaves (for flavour)
3 eggs
150 ml (¼ pint) single cream
150 ml (¼ pint) milk

15 ml (1 tbsp) unrefined golden granulated sugar
freshly grated nutmeg

To serve
150 ml (¼ pint) fresh orange juice

Put the spinach leaves in a saucepan and cook them lightly in the water that clings to them after rinsing. Remove; allow to cool and squeeze out the juice into a bowl. Discard the spinach pulp and keep the juice.

Rinse the tansy leaves and put them in a blender with 15 ml (1 tbsp) water. Squeeze the tansy juice through a nylon sieve using a wooden spoon. Add it to the spinach juice. Discard the tansy pulp. Beat the juices with the eggs, cream, milk, sugar and nutmeg.

Oil 6 dariole moulds or a custard mould or ovenproof bowl and fill with the mixture. Bake in a water bath in the oven at 150°C (350°F) mark 2 for about 30 minutes, or until the custards are set. Leave to cool.

Slip a knife round the sides and turn the custards out on to individual plates and pour a little orange juice around them. Serve the juice separately if you made one large custard.

Peter Gandey, who buys and
sells the catch of Newhaven's

Food from the Sea

inshore fishing fleet, knows that there is much more to his business than the cod to go with the chips. There's gurnard and John Dory, whiting, ling, and conger. And that's long before you start on the bass and red mullet, the lobsters and crabs, squid and deep-water scallops – let alone the herring, the mackerel and the sprats.

'I try to turn whatever the fleet lands into money,' Peter says with a grin. 'We go all over for our markets. In France the red gurnard is in demand. French fishermen take great care to preserve the colour: they cover the fish with skate-wings as the slime keeps the scarlet skin fresh. Grey gurnard in England is just used as bait – you can't give it away. But the golden gurnard can grow to 2.8–3.2 kg (6–7 lb), and it makes very good eating. In fact everything that comes from the sea is good eating. No one knew about monkfish in the old days. The gurnard is the monkfish of today – just waiting to be discovered.'

Peter no longer goes out with the fleet himself. Nowadays he contents himself with rod-and-line in Scotland, and some very serious deer stalking. Land and sea hunting require surprisingly similar skills. 'The commercial fisherman has to have a feel for the chase – an instinct for the quarry. A fish in good condition is harder to catch than one in poor condition. Some fish are cleverer than others. Plaice, for instance, are clever fish, and difficult to catch in clear water – they can see the trawl coming. Skate are "flighty" – you catch them in one area once and next time they are gone. Cod and conger shelter in wrecks against the strong tides in the Channel. A good fisherman has to pit his wits against the fish.'

Eight years ago Peter Gandey's partner, Peter Ellis, came off the boats to take care of direct sales to the hotel and restaurant trade: 'There's a new appetite for unusual fish today, the kind we used to be able to sell only on the Continent. People travel abroad and try new dishes. When they come home, they look for whatever they enjoyed on their holiday.'

Peter supplies local restaurateur John Kenward, chef/proprietor of the much-praised Kenward's in Lewes, a short distance inland. John is a hands-on, self-taught cook whose trademark is perfect ingredients, simply prepared. He does his own daily marketing and tailors his menu to the vagaries of the catch.

The sea and fishing are also very much a part of Cornish life, and Angela and Harry Thomas, who own and run Nansloe Manor, a small, comfortable country-house hotel with a busy restaurant on the outskirts of Helston, make the most of their local produce. 'Both my chef, Martin Jones, and I love cooking fish – we have wonderful crab and lobsters,' says Angela.

Down the coast in Mousehole, fisherman Phil Wallis's wife Audrey always has a tin of hevva cake handy to hand round with the cups of tea that greet all visitors. The Wallises are fishermen by birth. Audrey's grandson Carl is now the 'jouster' selling fish door-to-door from the van that replaced the pony and trap, counting Nansloe Manor among his customers.

Fisherman's Kettle

Stews like this have been made up and down the coast of Europe since the Vikings first put to sea.

Serves 4

1.4 kg (3 lb) whole white fish (flatfish, monkfish, gurnard, rock salmon, eel)	1.1 litres (2 pints) water
	1 glass white or rosé wine
	salt and white peppercorns
handful of mussels in the shell	25 g (1 oz) butter
handful of prawns	2 large potatoes
1 small bacon hock	2 egg yolks
2 small onions	30 ml (2 tbsp) single cream
small bunch of parsley	(optional)
1 bay leaf	

Get the fishmonger to skin and bone the fish – make sure he gives you all the trimmings. Cut all the larger fillets into bite-sized strips. Scrub and beard the mussels and pick over the prawns. Trim and cube all the good lean meat from the bacon hock.

Put the bacon bones and skin in a large fish kettle with the fish trimmings. Add a small onion (cut in half, but with the skin left on for colour), the parsley stalks, bay leaf, water, wine, salt and crushed peppercorns. Bring to the boil, turn down to simmer, cover and cook for 30 minutes. Strain the liquor, pressing out the juices, and return to the kettle.

Peel and finely slice the second onion. Cube the reserved bacon. Fry the onion and bacon gently in the butter in a small frying pan until they are well cooked and lightly browned.

Peel the potatoes and slice thickly. Bring the fish stock to the boil with the potatoes and simmer for 10–15 minutes until tender. Add the fish, firm-fleshed first, softer (flatfish) next and crustaceans and shellfish last. Bring all back to a bubble, turn down heat and poach for 2–3 minutes. Tip the contents of the frying pan into the kettle.

Beat the egg yolks with the cream if you are using it, and a ladleful of warm (not boiling) broth. Stir it into the kettle and return to the heat but do not re-boil. Serve in deep plates.

Fish Scouse

The scouse is the Fisherman's Kettle carried to its logical conclusion.

Serves 2

45–60 ml (3–4 tbsp) oil (plus bacon
    drippings if available)
6–8 leftover ladlesful drained from
    the Fisherman's Kettle (see page
    23)
salt and pepper

To serve
1 egg
chilli sauce

In a heavy frying pan, heat the oil and drippings. Tip in the drained fish and potato (it doesn't have to be bone-dry – in fact the flavour will be better if you leave quite a lot of liquid to evaporate).

Reduce the mixture gently over a low heat. As the liquid evaporates, so the base will begin to fry. Turn the crust over and continue to fry until another crust forms. Turn it again. Finally add salt and pepper.

When the scouse is deliciously crisped and brown, but still juicy, it is ready. Reheat it in the pan rather than keeping it warm. Serve it with a fried egg and a shake of chilli sauce.

Lemon Sole with Mussels and Leeks

Lemon sole, a speciality of Newhaven, is the most delicious of the plaice family, and usually good value for money. It's small for a flatfish – from 15–27.5 cm (6–11 inches) long. A little one on the bone will serve one. For his favourite recipe, John Kenward chose a large fish which he filleted to give two portions. Although Dover sole is skinned first and filleted later, lemon sole should be filleted first and then the fillets can easily be slipped off their skin with a sharp knife.

Serves 2

700 g (1½ lb) lemon sole on the
    bone
2 medium leeks
1 large carrot
1 garlic clove, skinned
2–3 fresh fennel fronds
small sprig rosemary or thyme

600 ml (1 pint) water
8–10 mussels
50 g (2 oz) butter
lemon juice
salt and pepper
15 ml (1 tbsp) olive oil for frying

Fillet the fish – or have your fishmonger do it for you. Make sure he gives you all the bones and trimmings.

Wash and trim the leeks, saving plenty of the green as well as the white. Slice the leeks into rings on the diagonal and wash them again. Chop the carrot into lengths. Crush the garlic.

Put the fish and leek rings, the chopped carrot, garlic and herbs into a saucepan, add the water, bring to the boil, then cover and simmer for 30 minutes to make a well-flavoured stock. Meanwhile, wash the mussels in plenty of fresh running water and scrub their shells. Put them in a sieve and balance the sieve over the boiling stock. Cover and cook them quickly in the steam until they open. Then put them to one side, shelled or unshelled as you prefer (if they are very sandy, shell them and rinse them off in a little of the stock).

Strain the solids from the stock (discard the last ladleful, which may still have some sand from the mussels in it), and boil the broth uncovered down to half its volume.

Melt half the butter in a small frying pan. When it foams, lay in the fish fillets and cook them for 2–3 minutes a side, until they are opaque and firm. Take out the fillets and lay them on warmed plates with the mussels.

Pour the broth into the pan and boil it up, scraping in any brown fishy bits. Bubble fiercely for a moment and then whisk in the rest of the cold butter, cut into little nuggets. Finish with a squeeze of lemon. Taste and add salt and pepper.

Pour the sauce round the fish on the warm plates. Heat the oil in the frying pan. Toss in the leeks and turn them in the hot oil. Divide the leeks between the plates, and serve immediately – the delicious fresh flavours will not improve with keeping.

Cod Fillets with Scallops and Cider

John Kenward's speciality is also good made with fresh haddock or fillets of flatfish. Mussels or prawns can replace the deep-water scallops, Newhaven's most sought-after delicacy.

Serves 4

700 g (1½ lb) fresh cod fillets
fish bones and skin for stock
½ onion, skinned and roughly chopped
1 celery stalk, roughly chopped
salt and black peppercorns

600 ml (1 pint) water
4 scallops
25 g (1 oz) butter
1 wine glass dry cider
100 g (4 oz) cold butter
½ lemon

Skin and fillet the fish – or have your fishmonger do this for you, but make sure he gives you the skin and some bones for the stock. Cut the fillets lengthways into two or three strips, and cut them again on the diagonal to give you pieces about the length of your hand.

Make a stock with the fish skin and bones, the onion and celery, a little salt, half a dozen crushed peppercorns and the water. Simmer the stock, uncovered, for 30 minutes until reduced to a well-flavoured 300 ml (½ pint). Strain out and discard all the solids. Reserve the liquid.

Open the scallops if they are still in the shell. Separate the white muscle and the coral roe and wash them well. Dry and slice each white muscle into two or three discs.

Melt 25 g (1 oz) butter in a frying pan. When the butter foams, slip in the discs of white scallop, no more than five or six pieces at a time or the temperature will drop and the fish will poach – it is this frying which gives the dish its flavour. Fry the pieces for 2–3 minutes, until they are browned at the edges, then put them in a dish to keep warm. Continue until the scallops and butter are used up, and you have plenty of brown sticky bits in the pan. Cook the roe at the very end briefly (but be careful not to split the membrane).

Lay the cod fillets in the pan and pour in enough cider and stock to poach them – the liquid should not quite cover the fish. Bring quickly to the boil. Then turn down the heat and simmer the fish uncovered for 3–5 minutes, depending on the thickness of the fillets. The unsubmerged top surface will whiten when they are done.

Take the fish out carefully and divide it between four warm plates. Increase the heat under the cooking liquid and bubble it up for a few minutes, to concentrate the flavour of the sauce. Make sure all the brown sticky bits are scraped in.

Beat the cold butter in small pieces into the sauce – warm it but do not overheat or the butter will oil (a spoonful of cold water will bring it back). Add a squeeze of lemon, taste and adjust the seasoning, and put in the scallops to warm through for a moment. Pour the sauce round the fish on the warm plates, and garnish with the scallops.

Baked Crab with Lemon

This Nansloe Manor recipe is a very good one for frozen or even tinned crab. Fresh crab is so delicious it doesn't need any help at all.

Serves 4

700 g (1½ lb) crabmeat	salt and pepper
25 g (1 oz) butter	
25 g (1 oz) plain flour	To finish
150 ml (¼ pint) double cream	50 g (2 oz) grated cheese
300 ml (½ pint) milk	pinch of paprika
30 ml (2 tbsp) lemon juice	1 lemon, quartered
a little grated lemon rind	

Pick over the crab to remove shell fragments (let it thaw completely if it was frozen). Melt the butter in a small saucepan. Stir in the flour and cook for 1 minute. Pour in the cream and milk, whisking over heat to avoid lumps. Season and simmer for 10 minutes. Add the lemon juice and rind to taste – when it is right, add the crab. Don't break up the meat – keep it chunky.

Divide the mixture between four cleaned crab shells, scallop shells or individual ovenproof dishes. Sprinkle with cheese and paprika. Reheat in the oven if necessary, but don't overcook. When you are ready to serve, pop the dishes under a very hot grill for a few minutes to add flavour and colour. Serve bubbling hot, with lemon quarters.

Scallops in Saffron Sauce

This is a favourite recipe of Martin Jones, chef at Nansloe Manor at Helston in Cornwall. He says that the lovely earthy scent of the saffron enhances the sea-scent of the scallops.

Serves 4 as a first course, 2 as a main course

24 medium scallops
1 small knob of butter
150 ml (¹/₄ pint) white wine
150 ml (¹/₄ pint) fish stock (made
   with the bones and trimmings
   from turbot and sole – any fish
   except plaice, which turns the
stock bitter – plus bay leaf,
carrot, onion, leek, celery. Boil,
skim, simmer, then strain off the
liquid and reduce by two-thirds)
30 ml (2 tbsp) thick double cream
about 12 saffron strands
salt (optional)

With a small knife, go into the hinges of the scallops and lever the shells apart.

Heat a small, deep frying pan, add the butter and sauté the scallops for about 2 minutes in all – if you cook them for any length of time they toughen up, so they should still be raw on the inside. Remove from the pan and keep warm.

Splash in the white wine and bubble it up, scraping in the flavoursome bits from the sauté. Reduce by two-thirds. Add the fish stock and reduce it by a further third. Stir in the cream and the saffron. Simmer, without boiling, stirring regularly, for about 10 minutes over a gentle heat, until the sauce coats the back of the wooden spoon. Add salt if you like – but take care not to destroy the delicate flavours.

Arrange the scallops, either in their own shells, or in shell-shaped dishes, and pour the sauce over them.

Gurnard with Orange Butter

Gurnard is an undiscovered culinary delight in Britain – an odd angular fish with a large bony head, slender body and long whisker-like feelers under the throat. John Kenward's recipe.

Serves 4

1.8–2.3 kg (4–5 lb) golden gurnard
zest and juice of 1 small orange
100 g (4 oz) butter, softened
30 ml (2 tbsp) chopped fresh
   tarragon

salt and freshly ground black
   pepper
aromatic oil (see page 30)

Clean, wipe and skin the fish. The skinning is easily done by you or your fishmonger: take a sharp knife and cut off the top fin down the full length of the body, trimming right into the flesh. Cut off the bottom fin in the same way, from the belly cavity down to the tail. Cut through the backbone, going in with a cut just behind the head. Grip the head firmly in one hand – it will still be attached to the body by the gills – and pull it down towards the tail. The skin will come off like a glove. Trim off the tail.

Beat the orange juice into the butter, then beat in the zest and the tarragon. Keep the orange butter in the refrigerator until you are ready to cook the fish.

Season the skinned fish with salt and pepper and rub it lightly with aromatic oil. Wrap in cooking foil and bake in the oven at 190°C (375°F) mark 5 for 25 minutes. Check to see if it is cooked through by lifting the flesh at the backbone. When it comes away easily, you know it is ready. Serve with a knob of orange butter to melt into the firm sweet flesh.

Brill with Aromatic Oil

Close cousin to the turbot but considerably cheaper, brill is a fine, firm-fleshed fish, at its best cooked simply.

Serves 4

1 whole brill, about 1.4–1.8 kg (3–4 lb)
1 small bottle olive oil flavoured with fennel, lovage or samphire (see below)

2–3 sprigs fennel, lovage or samphire

Wipe and gut the fish but leave it whole. Rub it all over with aromatic oil, salt it generously and tuck the fennel, lovage or samphire into the belly cavity.

Heat a heavy iron grill pan smoking hot. Place the fish on it (or you can cook it under the grill or on a barbecue). If the fish is as thick as a thumb, cover it loosely with a lid to speed up the cooking process. Turn it over and cook the other side. It is done when the flesh is opaque and a fork just lifts it easily from the backbone. Fillet the fish at the table straight on to warm plates. Serve with a little aromatic oil.

AROMATIC OIL

Aromatic oil is easily made: completely immerse a sprig of your chosen herb in a bottle of good olive oil. Leave it to infuse for a week or two. The infused oil does not have a long shelf-life – keep it in the fridge and use within a month. Sunflower is better if you want it to last.

Spring in the Garden of England

Shuttle down to the Channel ports and you scarcely notice the county of Kent. The noisy motorway traffic thunders through her apple and cherry orchards and past the tip-hatted oast-houses. Blink and you'll miss the towering hop-poles, the strawberry fields and market gardens, which traditionally supply London with early vegetables. Channel commuters have no time to take a leisurely detour to pick up a crate of oysters from the reseeded beds of Whitstable or a barrel of Shepherd Neame's beer, or to admire the flocks cropping the sea-scented pastures of Romney Marsh.

The people of Kent are used to travellers passing through. This, after all, is the highway to the Continent. William the Conqueror's soldier-sailors marched down the arrow-straight road, its foundations laid by Caesar's legionaries who spat out imported cherry stones which took root in Kentish soil. It takes time to put down roots, and the natives of the garden of England continue to draw strength and permanence from their own good earth.

Graham Cooper, butcher to the people of Aldington, south of Ashford, takes pride in his roots. He has lived all his life in the cottage he shares with his wife Sylvia, art-student daughter Melanie and trainee cabinet-maker son Christopher. 'There have been Coopers in Kent for more generations than anyone can remember,' he says.

Graham started in the trade aged 11, doing Saturday morning deliveries with his dad. 'My father studied his craft at Smithfield. He always bought the best-in-show – people would order their Christmas beef off the best-in-show. Sales were all local then, within a 10-mile radius. We bought our first van just after the war; before then we delivered by pony-and-trap. My grandfather was a horse-breaker for New Forest and Welsh ponies. Butchering and horses always used to go together: you have to know how to handle livestock.

31

'People have forgotten how to buy meat: they go to supermarkets and look at packets and don't know what they're buying. People eat less meat: no more huge weekend joints roast on Sunday, cold on Monday, done up on Tuesday and Wednesday. It was an economical way and saved labour. Before the First World War people used to buy 10 to 12 pounds of meat, along with half a pound of suet for the dumplings, to last the week out. And that was it.

'Nowadays, people want convenience. They come in with a basket and like to find everything they need. People come in, pick up a packet, read the recipe on the back, and then come over and ask for the meat. They're packet-led. And if they don't get what they want from us they go down to the supermarket and get everything there, including the meat. Butchers need to know something about cooking or they can't talk about the meat or know what's needed for a particular recipe.'

Before long the Channel Tunnel will disgorge a new wave of invaders to swell the traffic on the old Roman road. Whitstable may once again export its oysters to Rome, Canterbury lamb rival the *présalé* of Normandy in the restaurants of Paris.

Four-Way Oysters

It's very nice to see the oyster beds at Seasalter by Whitstable in Kent once again productive (they were knocked out of action early this century).

If you can't handle an oyster-knife, cheat by putting the oysters in the freezer for about 12 hours, then defrost them for 1½ hours and the shells will open. Farmed oysters can safely be eaten all year round.

Serves 4

24 oysters
  (6 for each variation)
lemon wedges

For the oysters Kilpatrick
cold butter
Worcester sauce
3–4 crisp-fried rashers of bacon

For the oysters au gratin
chopped fresh parsley and chives
a drop of Pernod or gin
a little cream
breadcrumbs

grated Parmesan
knob of butter

For the oysters with chilli
15 ml (1 tbsp) wine vinegar
5 ml (1 tsp) tomato purée
15 ml (1 tbsp) olive oil
1 fresh green chilli, deseeded and
  chopped, or 2.5 ml (1 tsp)
  cayenne
5 ml (1 tsp) paprika
1 garlic clove, skinned and crushed
5 ml (1 tsp) finely chopped onion
pinch of salt

Serve six of the oysters raw with lemon. For the oysters Kilpatrick: open the oysters and lay them in the deep shell on the grill tray (take care not to lose any of the delicious juices). Top each with a tiny sliver of butter, a dash of Worcester sauce and the crumbled bacon. Grill for 2 minutes.

For the oysters au gratin: top each oyster on the half shell with parsley, chives, a drop of Pernod or gin and a dab of cream. Finish with a hat of breadcrumbs and grated Parmesan and a sliver of butter. Grill for 2 minutes to gild the topping.

For the oysters with chilli: mix all the ingredients to make a sauce. Spoon on to the oysters and grill for 2 minutes.

Creamed Spinach with Nutmeg

If preferred, you can cook the spinach in the microwave; it gives perfect results and none of the flavour is lost.

Serves 4

450 g (1 lb) spinach
1.25 ml (¼ tsp) grated nutmeg

150 ml (¼ pint) single cream
salt and pepper

Lightly boil the spinach, for about 4 minutes, in the water that clings to the leaves after washing (early spinach is grown in sand so needs thorough rinsing). Drain, chop and mix in the nutmeg and cream. Season to taste.

Vegetables with Herb Cream

In springtime, after the heavy stews and root vegetables of winter, there's no better way to start a meal than with a dish of tiny Kent-grown vegetables, cooked lightly and plainly.

Serves 4

150 ml (¼ pint) whipping cream
15 ml (1 tbsp) mild mustard
generous handful of fresh herbs,
    including parsley
4–6 spring onions
salt
900 g (2 lb) (total weight) mixed
    young vegetables: choose new

potatoes, baby beetroot with
leaves still attached, baby
carrots, young green beans, baby
leeks, asparagus sprue or hop
shoots, if you can find them (they
used to be popular in Kent), baby
courgettes, sugar peas

Mix the lightly whipped cream with the mustard and stir in the chopped herbs and spring onions. Taste and add salt. Trim and rinse the vegetables, removing any discoloured leaves, but leaving them as whole as possible.

Cook the new potatoes in a saucepan of boiling water. They will take 8–18 minutes, depending on size. Do not overcook; drain them immediately. Meanwhile bring a large saucepan of salted water to the boil. Cook the other vegetables for a few minutes only. Tiny carrots and whole baby courgettes need 5–6 minutes. Baby beetroot will need longer. Baby leeks need 3–4 minutes after they come back to the boil. The young shoots, beans and sugar peas need only to be blanched, i.e. brought back to the boil and drained.

Arrange the well-drained vegetables on a warm dish and serve them with the cream sauce.

Crown Roast of Romney Marsh Lamb

Sylvia has a few general rules for cooking meat: look at the joint and see how much fat there is. The more fat, the longer cooking time it needs, so start a fatty joint high and turn it low, then cook it longer and increase the heat at the end to crisp the fat. If the meat's too lean it dries out, so ask the butcher to tie an extra piece of fat round it. Remember that lean meat toughens if it's cooked on too high a heat.

Serves 4

1 crown roast with 8 cutlets and all its trimmings

handful of parsley and sprigs of thyme, roughly chopped
freshly ground pepper (no salt)

Let the meat come up to room temperature. Top the bones with 'pearls' – rolled balls of fat – to protect them from charring.

Put aside the circle of fat your butcher will have popped in the middle of the crown. Chop up the rest of the trimmings; mix them with the herbs and pepper and use this to fill the middle. Top it with the fat circle.

Preheat the roasting pan – meat shouldn't start in cold metal. Roast the meat in the oven at 180°C (350°F) mark 4 for 15–20 minutes per 450 g (1 lb).

Serve on a hot dish and use well-warmed plates, as lamb fat solidifies quickly. Serve with minted peas – a fine crop of which is grown side by side with the flocks on the Marsh – and the traditional accompaniments for lamb.

LAMB

Romney Marsh Sheep-breeding Society exports stock animals all over the world, including to the Falklands. Lamb is 'milk-fed' as long as it's still on its mother: once it's grazing, it becomes ordinary lamb. At a year old – around Christmas in Kent – it's a hogget. To a butcher the difference is visible: apart from size, the hogget's fat is pure white and the meat coarser-grained and darker.

Redcurrant and Port-wine Jelly

Strip the currants from their stalks and put them in a saucepan with enough water to cover. Boil for about 20 minutes until setting point is reached. Mash them with a potato masher and strain out the solids (or leave them in, if you prefer). Stir in sugar to taste – about 450 g (1 lb) for each 450 g (1 lb) of fruit. Bring gently back to the boil, stirring to dissolve the crystals. Cook it for 5 minutes, then put aside to cool. Stir in a sherry glass of port wine for each 1.1 litres (2 pints) of jelly. Bottle and seal as usual. Serve with lamb.

Beef in Ale

Serves 4

700 g (1½ lb) chuck steak cut into large bite-sized pieces

25 g (1 oz) flour seasoned with 1.25 ml (¼ tsp) pepper and 15 ml (1 tbsp) dried mixed herbs

1 large onion, skinned and chopped

350 g (12 oz) old carrots, scraped and sliced

1 bottle (275 ml) brown ale

Toss the meat in the seasoned and herbed flour. Put it in a casserole dish with the onion and carrots. Mix well. Pour in the ale. Cover tightly and cook in a slow steady oven at 150°C (300°F) mark 2 for 4 hours.

Horseradish Cream

Fresh horseradish root is very fiery. Later in the year, the root dries out underground, and it will absorb more cream.

Makes 2 small jars

225 g (8 oz) fresh horseradish root
150 ml (¼ pint) carton single cream
15 ml (1 tbsp) white wine or cider
   vinegar

5 ml (1 tsp) mustard powder
2.5 ml (½ tsp) ground black
   mustard

Grate the horseradish; the fumes sting your eyes, so this is best done in a food processor. Mix in enough cream to cover the shavings. Add the vinegar slowly to the mustard powder and ground mustard, then stir into the horseradish. Store in a screw-top jar. It keeps for 3 months in the refrigerator.

Fresh from the Fells

In the spectacular Cumbrian lake country an ancient tradition of hospitality has resulted in a high concentration of good restaurants and comfortable hotels catering for the ever-swelling river of tourists who start arriving at this time of year.

Cumbria's culinary strengths depend on its fine home-grown ingredients. Lamb from the local breed of Herdwick sheep goes into the dinner-time stew pot. In recent years several of the old water-powered mills have been restored to produce the vigorous mixed-grain flours characteristic of hill-farming areas. There is also a fine repertoire of pork specialities, including rich dark slabs of black pudding and snail-coils of juicy Cumberland sausage.

In true Cumbrian tradition, former restaurateur Joyce Woodcock cut her culinary milk teeth in the hotel her parents ran in Borrowdale. Between them they acquired and ran the Park End Restaurant in Caldbeck, an enterprise that soon earned the family team a formidable local reputation, until she married Richard, who ran the local garage. Now they have their own garage with a house attached, and are seriously thinking about getting a small hotel and restaurant to run.

Hearing the children scrambling over the wall on their way home for lunch Joyce pulls a tatie pot out of the oven and takes it over to the table. Savoury steam fills the kitchen and the scent draws Richard to the dinner table. Joyce ladles out meat, potatoes and dark gravy enriched with black pudding.

'In the old days, in my grandmother's time, the kids had to walk over the fell to school. Each took a tatie with their initials carved into it, and the taties went into the ashes at the bottom of the stove in the schoolroom. By lunch-time they were ready. What could be better?'

Tatie Pot

The Tatie Pot, Joyce says, is the huntsmen's favourite dish. John Peel lived in Caldbeck, and his hunt, the Blencathra, is just down the way. Tatie Pot is best started a day ahead so you can lift off the fat when it has set.

Serves 4

1.6 kg (3½ lb) neck of lamb on the bone, chopped

1–2 medium onions, skinned and sliced

3–4 carrots, scraped and roughly sliced

1 large swede or turnip, peeled and chopped into bite-size pieces

450 g (1 lb) black pudding (in skin or piece), sliced

900 g (2 lb) potatoes, peeled and thinly sliced

salt and pepper

Put the lamb, onion, carrots and swede or turnip into a baking tray. Cover with boiling water and season.

Bring everything back to the boil. Cover with foil. Cook in the oven at 130°C (250°F) mark 1 for 4–5 hours until the softened meat falls off the bone easily. Ladle out the juice and leave it to get cold, preferably overnight. Lift off and retain the hat of fat.

Bone and cut the meat into bite-sized chunks. Arrange the meat and vegetables back in the baking tray. Cover with black pudding. Boil up the juices, taste and adjust the seasoning, and pour over the meat so that it comes right to the top. Lay overlapping discs of potato over the top. Dot with lamb fat. Season, cover with foil, and return the dish to a hot oven, 190°C (375°F) mark 5, to bake for 50–60 minutes. Remove the foil after 30–40 minutes, when the potatoes are soft, to crisp and gild them at the edges.

Serve with Pickled Red Cabbage (see page 41).

Cumberland Sausage with Apple Sauce

Joyce gets her sausages and black puddings from John Stevenson of Browtop Farm at Hutton Roof near Skelton. John was a pig farmer, but found the new regulations made the business of rearing the animals uneconomic. Now turned pork-butcher, he calls round the area in his van selling meat.

Serves 4

700 g (1½ lb) Cumberland sausage (this is a pure pork sausage, not twisted into links, but left curled into a snail)
25 g (1 oz) lard or dripping
1 small baking apple, cored and washed (leave the skin on)

For the apple sauce
450 g (1 lb) Bramley apples
juice of ½ lemon
25 g (1 oz) butter

Put the coil of sausage, with a small baking apple in the eye of the curl, in a baking tin. Prick it with a fork and dot with lard or dripping. Bake in the oven at 180°C (350°F) mark 4 for 50–60 minutes until the juices run clear. This sausage is best done in the oven, as it is too meaty to grill or fast fry.

Make the apple sauce: peel, core and slice the apples and put them in a small saucepan with the lemon juice and a splash of water. Bring to the boil, cover and simmer for 15–20 minutes until the apples have fallen into a snowy mush. Beat in the butter.

Serve the sausage with potatoes sautéed in the pan drippings, surrounded by a selection of seasonal vegetables. Hand round some Cumberland mustard and the apple sauce to accompany them.

Pickled Red Cabbage

Makes 1.4 kg (3 lb)

900 g (2 lb) red cabbage
15 ml (1 tbsp) salt
2–3 slices raw beetroot (for extra colour)

2–3 slices raw onion (for extra flavour)
600 ml (1 pint) cider vinegar
5 ml (1 tsp) pickling spice

Slice the cabbage into fine ribbons, spread it in a shallow dish, and salt it thoroughly. Leave overnight. Next day, drain it and pack into jars. Top each jar with a slice of beetroot and onion.

Boil up the vinegar and spices and simmer for 15 minutes. Strain this over the cabbage and seal the pots. It will be ready in a month – but you can eat it after a week.

This sharp-flavoured, rosy pickle, which cuts the richness of meat, is the traditional companion for Tatie Pot (see page 39).

A Mail-order Feast

'When you live in rural Hert-fordshire, you can't just pop down to the shops for something delicious. So we plan ahead and do it all on the telephone,' Anne Grimsdale, a second-generation market-researcher, says with a smile.

The Grimsdale family – Anne shares a house in the village of Anstey with her mother Pauline and father Len – have a fine appreciation of the good things in life but they work hard for them, since the outer rim of the M25, they say, is pretty much a gastronomic desert.

Quality is the key to the Grimsdales' selection of their mail-order suppliers. 'We like good food. It's more important than quantity.'

The household has an order of meat delivered every six weeks or so from Heal Farm in Devon, where livestock expert Anne Petch has established a national reputation by pioneering the production of naturally reared meats from traditional breeds.

A deep-freeze is essential to the dedicated mail-order cook, although postal shopping still tends to reflect the seasons. Spring, summer, autumn and winter each have their specialities, and are all delivered to the door.

Far from being impersonal, luxury mail-order depends on a good relationship between supplier and supplied: the proof of the pudding, and half the fun, is in the unwrapping.

For the Grimsdales, mail order is the answer to the vanishing purveyor of high-class groceries. Perfect presentation of the goods, impeccable packaging and reliability of carrier are the keys to a happy partnership.

The following recipes comprise a typical mail-order party feast.

Brawn with Pears

Brawn is a neglected delicacy. When well-made with cider and plenty of parsley, it's just as good as the French *fromage de tête*. Heal Farm's pig-cheek brawn has a light set and comes in small tubs. Butcher's brawn is usually firm enough to slice. Serve with slivers of fresh fruit and a mustardy vinaigrette.

Serves 4 as a starter

225 g (8 oz) brawn
30 ml (2 tbsp) chopped fresh
**   parsley**
1–2 firm pears

For the dressing
10 ml (2 tsp) wholegrain mustard
5 ml (1 tsp) grated horseradish
10 ml (2 tsp) tarragon wine vinegar
60 ml (4 tbsp) olive oil
salt and pepper

Tip the brawn out on to a pretty plate and sprinkle with chopped parsley. Fork together the mustard, horseradish and vinegar and work in the olive oil until you have a nice thick *rémoulade*. Season with salt and pepper. Flank the brawn with pear segments, then trickle the dressing over the fruit.

Ham with Fresh Pickled Peaches

Combining ham with spiced or pickled peaches is traditional in British cooking. This recipe uses ready-cooked ham.

Serves 4 as a starter

225 g (8 oz) finely sliced ham
1–2 peaches
30 ml (2 tbsp) white wine vinegar
2.5 ml (1/2 tsp) fresh or dried ginger

pinch of ground cloves
chopped fresh mint (optional)
pepper

Serve the sliced ham with a relish of sliced peach dressed with the vinegar and spices and finished with the optional mint. The peach perfectly complements the sweet firm flesh of the ham. Apples, pears, mango, even bananas (finished with toasted coconut) would make an alternative to peaches.

Smoked Pork Tenderloin with Mango

Smoked pork tenderloin can be served raw, as here, or it can be cooked like veal escalopes – beaten, breadcrumbed and fried, or sautéed in butter and finished with cream and cider.

Serves 4 as a starter

225 g (8 oz) smoked pork tenderloin (or smoked ham)

1 apple, cored and cut into thin segments

1 small mango, skinned and cut into thin segments

juice of 1 lemon, plus pieces of lemon to garnish

1.25 ml (¼ tsp) ground cumin

salt and pepper

Slice the fillet on the diagonal, to give thin medallions. Interleave the slices alternately with segments of apple and mango, arranged on a pretty plate. Dress the fruit and meat with plenty of lemon juice to keep the fruit from browning – and to give definition to the smoked pork tenderloin, which has a very mild flavour.

Before serving, sprinkle with a pinch of cumin, season with salt and pepper and finish with a piece of lemon to garnish.

Pork Seville

Seville 'marmalade' oranges give the best flavour to this dish; if they are not available, use thin-skinned juice oranges.

Serves 4–6

700 g (1½ lb) lean pork, diced (shoulder is best)

2 oranges

50 g (2 oz) dried apple rings

600 ml (1 pint) wine (red or white)

5 ml (1 tsp) dried tarragon

3 cloves

salt and pepper

15 ml (1 tbsp) arrowroot or 30 ml (2 tbsp) flour

Trim the meat, if necessary, and put in a bowl. Make the marinade: squeeze the juice from one orange and finely pare the zest. Thinly slice the other orange and set aside a few slices for garnishing. Mix the oranges with the apple rings, wine, tarragon, cloves, salt and pepper, pour the mixture over the pork and leave overnight to marinate.

Tip everything into a large casserole. Bring it gently to simmering point on top of the stove, then cook in the oven at 150°C (300°F) mark 3 for 2½ –3 hours. You can thicken the sauce towards the end of the cooking time with the arrowroot or flour mixed with a little water and stirred well in.

Lamb with Apricot and Nut Stuffing

Anne Grimsdale serves this joint with big flat mushrooms cooked in olive oil with garlic.

Serves 6–8

1 boned shoulder of lamb, weighing 1.8–2.3 kg (4–5 lb)
15 ml (1 tbsp) olive oil
1 garlic clove
15 ml (1 tbsp) flour
salt and pepper

For the stuffing
50 g (2 oz) dried apricots, stoned and chopped
50 g (2 oz) cashew nuts
100 g (4 oz) fresh breadcrumbs, soaked and squeezed
15 ml (1 tbsp) chopped fresh herbs
1 egg
salt and pepper

Lay the lamb on a table, cut-side up. Make a nice deep pocket for the stuffing, mix together all the stuffing ingredients and pack the pocket with a ball of the mixture. Fold the meat up over the stuffing and tie it up with string, like a parcel. Carry the string on round the lamb, making a wheel-spoke pattern.

Turn the joint so that the untidy side is underneath, and put in a roasting tin. Rub the meat with oil and a garlic clove cut in two, then dust with flour. Season.

Weigh the joint and calculate the cooking time at 15 minutes per 450 g (1 lb) plus 15 minutes. Roast the joint in the oven at 200°C (400°F) mark 6 for 10 minutes, then turn the heat down to 180°C (350°F) mark 4.

THE WEDDING BREAKFAST

My three bachelor daughters have not yet announced their nuptials, but the youngest at least has declared a commitment to white weddings, old lace and blue garters and I realise that where there are single daughters, the mother-of-the-bride will not be far behind. And mothers-of-the-bride, however floral-hatted and misty-eyed, worry about the wedding breakfast.

The British response to celebration meals is to whip up a sea of ham mousse and decorate it with limp slices of cucumber. There must surely be a more glorious gateway to the odyssey of marriage than a paper plate piled with characterless pink fluff.

Country cooks in other parts of Europe certainly think so: a wedding breakfast is an opportunity to prepare the family's own favourite dishes, but with the best possible ingredients. Rural cooks of the Mediterranean bring out the best of the larder stores – salt-dried ham and sausages, well-matured cheeses and homemade liqueurs – and their local bakery makes a special batch of loaves. The traditional Provençal wedding breakfast is a *Soupe de Mariage*. This is a simple boiled dinner of mixed meats: beef-shin, a shoulder of lamb or mutton, and a chicken are simmered together in the household's largest cooking pot (a tall, lidded earthenware *marmite*) with root vegetables and herbs. The old vegetables are removed after the slow cooking and replaced with new fresh ones. The soup, strained then simmered with aphrodisiac saffron and fortifying rice, is served first, then the meat and vegetables with little dishes of relishes – garlic mayonnaise, fresh tomato sauce, pickled cucumber, capers, a sharp herb-laden vinaigrette, rough salt.

In Eastern Europe, daily bread is enriched to make a bride-cake – using fine white flour instead of everyday rye, plus butter, eggs and dried fruit. Driving through the little shuttered villages of rural Transylvania in 1985, I joined a procession of country people in their brightly embroidered Sunday best, trundling a loaded flower-decked cart. The cart turned through double doors into a large farm courtyard walled with barns. Here in the afternoon sunlight, preparations for the wedding were in full swing: responsibility for the wedding banquet is divided between the families of both groom and bride. The festivities were to start at the groom's house: noodle soup made with chicken and beef broth would be served first, followed by the meats themselves, re-roasted with garlic, parsley, bay and dill. The procession I had joined was the bride's family bringing its required contribution – sugar-decorated sweetened breads, biscuits, nuts and apples.

After midnight the bride's party, plus the bridegroom, would leave the groom's guests to their dancing, and adjourn to the bride's house, where a wedding breakfast of paprika chicken had been prepared.

In rural Scandinavia, where farms and small communities were until recently quite isolated, guests at such a celebration each bring a dish for the *smörgasbord* table. This allows the cook to demonstrate her skills and taste the specialities of her neighbours, and avoids undue strain on any one family's larder stores – vital to survival in the harsh climate. Such meals are taken leisurely, with plenty of time for a *skol* drunk in beer.

So when your daughter decides to be bachelor no more, make the great day memorable by reviving the good, old-fashioned wedding breakfast. Serve *Soupe de Mariage* and herb-roasted meat, and eat under the trees.

SUMMER

High summer brings full–flavoured pleasures.

Long twilights and holiday time encourage everyone to get out and about, and the nicest way to enjoy your meals is alfresco. Even city dwellers can take to the parks and gardens.

At this time of year no one wants to spend all day slaving over a hot stove – even so, a little holiday leisure, particularly if you stay at home, gives an opportunity to cook for pleasure – maybe try a new skill. Anyone who has never baked their own bread is missing out on a real treat – it's a thoroughly primitive pleasure, and the easiest of all culinary skills to master. Children enjoy helping with dough pummelling and shaping, so it can be a family entertainment. Yeast works more quickly in the warmth of summer, and home-made loaves and rolls provide the backbone of simple, easily prepared meals.

A picnic tea is nicest with home-made cookies, cakes and buns – children love to help make sweet treats, and results are quickly achieved. Cake-making was the first culinary skill I acquired – although in my time, with post-war rationing still in force, ingredients were harder to come by, and butter and sugar a real luxury.

My own children's childhood was spent in the wilds of southern Spain where we enjoyed the pleasures of Moorish-inspired cooking – saffron and rice and magnificent vegetables. I still return for visits, and back in Britain, much of our family summer cooking makes use of those Mediterranean flavours. Even when the weather is not as perfect as memory suggests, you can still set a sunny table. Tomatoes make a delicious chilled soup for a soft evening in the damp Hebrides, roasted peppers lighten a long Norfolk twilight, and stuffed artichokes slow-cooked with olive oil bring back the warmth of sun-baked shores.

The fishing villages of the Norfolk coast bring in a harvest of flatfish, sea-trout, mullet – all at their best cooked simply and served with samphire which grows wild on the mud-flats. Generations of children have shrimped on wide flat shores, and a whole industry once gathered cockles and whelks to supply Londoners with the favourite street-snack. Inshore gathering provides a shellfish chowder in as little time as it take to steam the shells open.

My husband's family comes from the Western Isles of Scotland, and we have spent many rainy summers appreciating the pleasures of cooking fresh ingredients locally gathered – shellfish and seafood and garden vegetables make light and delicious dishes quickly and easily prepared. In the busy kitchen at Tiroran, just round the coast from my father-in-law's cottage on Mull, chef-proprietor Sue Blockey uses wild oysters to stuff a shoulder of local lamb, and gathers watercress to make a green sauce for locally-caught prawns.

Across the Irish sea, a sophisticated picnic for a summer evening at the opera serves as a reminder that alfresco eating in the grand manner was a luxury enjoyed by our grandparents. All it takes is time, a way with haute-cuisine, and a well-appointed hamper – plus an old-fashioned, white-gloved butler to hand it all round. Ah well: you can always dream – and call for a volunteer Jeeves.

So set your summer table with a bowl of roses, don't forget the brolly, and enjoy the full-blown pleasures of the richest season of the year.

Loch-side Cooking

Near Ben More on the Hebridean Isle of Mull stands a handsome stone-built Georgian house. To see it is to fall instantly in love with it – even if, as in the case of Sue and Robin Blockey, you first come across it in the middle of winter. Over the 15 years the Blockeys have lived there, the love affair has developed into a very contented working partnership and they run Tiroran as a hotel.

During the season (mid-May to end of September), Tiroran accommodates 17 guests. Even though others refer to it as 'the leisure business', there's nothing leisurely about the daily chores of a hotelier. 'We have help from six girls on a rota, sharing the waitressing, vegetable preparation and cleaning, but Robin and I do the rest,' Sue explains. 'I hate tantrums and waste. Otherwise I'm easy.' Her day begins at 5 a.m. The view from the downstairs bedroom offers some consolation for the early start. Below the window, the woodland garden meanders down a rocky glen to the glittering waters of Loch Scridain. Beyond is the headland of Ardmeanach, its jagged cliffs softened by a cloak of bracken and heather starred with harebells.

It runs with the precision of an officers' mess – Robin was a Wing Commander in the RAF before the move to Mull. Such precision may seem disconcerting, considering the usual gentle pace of the island, but there's no doubt that high-class catering on an island needs organisation. The usual staples are not a problem. If the Blockeys run out of sugar they can nip round the bay and pick up a packet in the shop. Egg-basket empty? The chickens scratching at the end of the rose-garden should be able to oblige and the Blockeys also keep a flock of American Indian Cayuga ducks whose eggs are a glorious shade of blue. But should they run out of extra-virgin olive oil for the watercress mayonnaise, they're stuck until someone comes over from the mainland.

Diana Warwick, who lives in a cottage up the way, is the kitchen's stalwart. She helps with the washing-up and keeps Sue supplied with fresh herbs. 'A few years ago I had a serious illness and realised what growing old might be like, so I put the flower and vegetable garden down to wild flowers and growing herbs for Tiroran,' Diana explains.

The garden provides gooseberries and blackberries and white, red and blackcurrants for summer treats. There are prawns in the bay; oysters for Sue to gather on the shore; watercress in the stream; fine fresh vegetables from John and Val's market garden at Glengorm to the north of the island. And, of course, there's tender lamb from the island's thyme-carpeted hill pastures.

Add to that the sparkle of the stream down the wooded brae, and it's hard to believe the snows of winter ever shroud Ben More, or sea-mist could haze the waters of Loch Scridain. But that, the Blockeys would confirm, is what falling in love is all about.

Tomato and Courgette Soup

Sue Blockey makes this soup with grilled tomatoes left over from breakfast.

Serves 4

225 g (8 oz) tomatoes
5 ml (1 tsp) sugar
salt and pepper
5 ml (1 tsp) chopped fresh basil
50 g (2 oz) butter
1 smallish onion, skinned and
   sliced

450 g (1 lb) courgettes, thinly sliced
1 glass red wine
600 ml (1 pint) milk or stock

To finish

150 ml (¼ pint) cream
5 ml (1 tsp) chopped fresh basil

Cook the tomatoes first: cut them in half, sprinkle lightly with sugar, salt and basil and top with a tiny knob of the butter. Put in the oven for 10 minutes until soft. This concentrates the flavour. Slip them out of their skins.

Sauté the onion and courgettes in the remaining butter. When they are soft, add the wine and skinned tomatoes and simmer for 10 minutes.

Whizz everything up in the food processor, turning it off before the mixture is quite smooth – a rough texture is nicer. Add the milk or stock. Season and chill well. Stir in the cream and sprinkle with fresh basil just before serving.

Prawns with Watercress Mayonnaise

Sue harvests watercress from her stream. There's plenty of it around in the wild, but make sure that it's growing in clean water.

Serves 6

900 g (2 lb) uncooked prawns
salt
30 ml (2 tbsp) white wine
5 ml (1 tsp) yeast extract, such as
   Marmite

For the mayonnaise
2 eggs
30 ml (2 tbsp) malt vinegar (including
   a dash of wine vinegar)

5 ml (1 tsp) grainy mustard
pinch of curry powder
handful watercress, plus a few
   sprigs to garnish
300 ml (½ pint) olive oil
300 ml (½ pint) sunflower oil
15 ml (1 tbsp) prawn glaze
   (see method)

Drop the prawns into boiling salted water. Bring them back to the boil and drain immediately. Let the prawns cool, then either peel them or serve them whole if you have extra prawn heads and carapaces to make the glaze.

For the glaze: mash the prawn heads and carapaces in a saucepan with a cupful of water, the wine and yeast extract. Reduce to 15 ml (1 tbsp) of liquid: strain and reserve.

Put the whole eggs (unseparated) into the food processor with the rest of the mayonnaise ingredients, except the oils and the prawn glaze. Turn on the machine at the speed you normally use to make mayonnaise. Gradually pour in the two oils until you have a properly thick emulsion. Add the prawn glaze. Serve the prawns with the mayonnaise and sprigs of watercress to garnish.

Lamb with Wild Oyster Stuffing

This dish can be made using farmed oysters which are available all year round.

Serves 4–6

1 boned shoulder of lamb, weighing
    1.8–2.3 kg (4–5 lb)
25 g (1 oz) butter

For the stuffing
6 oysters
100 g (4 oz) fresh breadcrumbs
6 anchovy fillets
4 rashers bacon
1 good handful parsley
1 egg
15 ml (1 tbsp) water
5 ml (1 tsp) crushed thyme
salt and pepper

For the sauce
6 oysters
25 g (1 oz) butter
25 g (1 oz) plain flour
300 ml (¹/₂ pint) creamy milk
5 ml (1 tsp) Worcester sauce
few drops of anchovy essence
pinch of cayenne

Unroll the boned shoulder of lamb and lay it flat on the table. Open the oysters for the stuffing and the sauce carefully, saving the liquor, and chop them roughly. Set aside half for the sauce.

Put the breadcrumbs to soak in the oyster liquor and crush the anchovies with a fork. Chop the bacon and the parsley and beat the egg lightly. Mix all the stuffing ingredients together.

Spread the stuffing over the meat. Roll it up and tie it securely. Season with salt and pepper. Melt the butter in a flameproof casserole that will just accommodate the joint. Turn the meat in the hot fat until it is lightly browned. Cover tightly and transfer to the oven. Cook at 190°C (375°F) mark 5 for about 1¹/₂ hours. Uncover for the last 10 minutes to brown the outside.

Meanwhile, make the sauce. Melt the butter and stir in the flour and milk. Season with Worcester sauce, a few drops of anchovy essence and a pinch of cayenne and heat, whisking continuously, until the sauce thickens, and is cooked. At the last moment tip in the oysters: they should be just immersed and warmed through, but not cooked or they go rubbery.

Taste and add salt and pepper plus any juices from the joint. Hand round the sauce with the lamb.

Variation For the stuffing, substitute 225 g (8 oz) button mushrooms for the oysters.

WILD OYSTERS

Sue gathers wild oysters when there is an 'r' in the month, from her own patch of shore – wild horses would not drag the exact location from her. To store the shellfish for summer sauces, she puts them in the deep-freeze as soon as she has gathered them, without shucking or scrubbing. Frozen oysters keep perfectly – and you don't have to struggle with an oyster knife when you defrost them, as shells conveniently gape open.

Potatoes Baked in a Chive Sauce

Sue thinks vegetables on their own can be very boring; 'they need a little sauce'.

Serves 4–6

900 g (2 lb) potatoes
1 garlic clove, skinned and chopped
salt and pepper
about 600 ml (1 pint) carrot water or
   chicken broth (home-made or
   from a stock cube)

15 ml (1 tbsp) English mustard
30 ml (2 tbsp) chopped chives

To finish
15 ml (1 tbsp) grated Parmesan
   cheese

Peel, slice and parboil the potatoes for 2 minutes, then drain. Grease a shallow casserole. Layer in the potato slices, sprinkling with chopped garlic and seasoning as you go.

Pour in enough broth, mixed with the mustard and chives, to come to the top of the potatoes. Dot the potatoes with butter, cover with foil, and bake in the oven at 190°C (375°F) mark 5 for 1 hour.

Take off the foil and sprinkle with grated Parmesan. Put the dish back in the oven for 10 minutes to brown and crust the potatoes.

Brown Bread and Cheese Buns

Sue reckons breadmaking is therapeutic, particularly if you're in a temper. She starts her bread first thing in the morning (about 8 am) and reckons to have it baking in the oven 1½ hours later.

Makes a 900 g (2 lb) loaf and a 450 g (1 lb) loaf, plus 18 small buns

550 g (1¼ lb) wholemeal flour
550 g (1¼ lb) strong plain flour
225 g (8 oz) malt flour
2 handfuls All-Bran
15 ml (1 tbsp) sesame seeds
75 g (3 oz) margarine
900 ml (1½ pints) warm milk
2 sachets easy blend dried yeast,
    enough to raise 1.4 kg (3 lb) flour
15 ml (1 tbsp) salt

For the buns
25 g (1 oz) butter
50 g (2 oz) grated cheese
30 ml (2 tbsp) finely chopped onion
30 ml (2 tbsp) dried mixed herbs or
    chopped parsley
1 egg, lightly beaten
15 ml (1 tbsp) sesame seeds

Put all the dough mixture into the bowl of the food mixer. Whizz it all up until it sticks to the beater. Take it out and pull it from side to side – left to right – to elasticate the dough.

Cut the lump of dough into three pieces, to give a 900 g (2 lb) loaf and a 450 g (1 lb) loaf, with the remaining piece reserved for the buns. Grease and flour the loaf tins, and settle in the dough. Cover the loaves and leave in a warm place until the dough rises and fills the tins.

Meanwhile make the buns. Roll out the remaining dough like pastry. Spread thinly with butter and sprinkle with cheese – enough to cover the dough. Scatter on half the onion and a pinch or two of herbs. Fold the dough over itself, roll it out and repeat the operation. Divide the dough into 18 pieces and roll into buns. Cover, and let them rise for 10 minutes. Brush with beaten egg and sprinkle with sesame seeds.

Bake the bread in the oven at 375°C (190°F) mark 5 for 35–45 minutes. Bake the buns in the oven at 220°C (425°F) mark 7 for 10 minutes.

Gooseberry Suédoise with Angelica

Sue is known as the pudding queen, adept at confections that round off a meal with a generous full stop. This delicate pale green gooseberry jelly is lovely in hot weather: the tart flavour of the berries is complemented by the sweet crisp meringue and smooth cream.

Serves 4–6

700 g (1½ lb) gooseberries
175 g (6 oz) granulated sugar (it
   dissolves better than caster)
600 ml (1 pint) water
handful of angelica stalks with
   leaves
15–25 g (½–1 oz) powdered
   gelatine

For the meringues
2 egg whites
5 ml (1 tsp) wine vinegar
100 g (4 oz) soft cane sugar

To finish
300 ml (½ pint) whipping cream
icing sugar

Top and tail the gooseberries and put them in a saucepan with the sugar and water and all but one 15–20 cm (6–8 inch) piece of angelica stalk. Simmer for 10 minutes, then remove from the heat and leave to infuse for 30 minutes to develop the flavours. Purée in a blender or food processor, then push through a sieve.

Measure the juice before reheating, and for every 600 ml (1 pint) stir in 15 g (½ oz) gelatine dissolved in a little hot water. Chop the reserved bit of angelica stalk very finely, and stir it in. Pour the jelly into a mould and leave to set.

Meanwhile make the meringues. Whisk the egg whites with the vinegar until they hold soft peaks (don't over-whisk or they go grainy). Beat in the sugar, spoon by spoon. Drop teaspoons (or use a star nozzle and piping bag) of the mixture on to an oiled and lightly floured baking sheet. Bake in the oven at 120°C (250°F) mark ½ for 45–50 minutes until the meringues are perfectly crisp.

Turn out the jelly and cover it with a thin layer of whipped cream, smoothed over with a palette knife. Finish with a hedgehog-coating of the little baby meringues. Decorate with a leafy sprig of angelica dipped in water and frosted with icing sugar.

Orange Shortbread

Feather light and deliciously buttery, shortbread is the great treat of the Scottish tea table. A 200 ml (7 fl oz) capacity teacup is used here.

Makes about 900 g (2 lb)

225 g (8 oz) unsalted butter,
   softened
1 teacup icing sugar
1 teacup cornflour

2 teacups plain flour
grated rind of 1 orange
a little caster sugar

Cream the butter with the icing sugar in a bowl, then knead in the flours and orange rind, using the tips of your fingers. Press the mixture into a shallow baking tin – it should be about 1 cm (½ inch) thick. Put it in the refrigerator for an hour to rest.

Bake in the oven at 180°C (350°F) mark 4 for 30 minutes. Take the shortbread out, prick it all over, and dust it with caster sugar. Reduce the oven temperature to 150°C (300°F) mark 2. Return the shortbread to the oven for 10 minutes to dry out.

Leave it to cool in the tin for 10 minutes, then turn out on to a wire rack.

Susan Elston and Julia Heffer # Take Two Norfolk Cooks

both love cooking. Best of all, they like cooking in each other's company. 'It's a joy,' Sue says. 'And two people together do the work of three. We've known each other for six years – since Julia moved here. We just looked in each other's kitchen cupboards, saw the mess and knew we were soulmates.'

Sue owns and runs Humble Pie, a high-class delicatessen and food shop in Market Place at Burnham Market in Norfolk. She first came here on holiday as a child and moved to Norfolk in 1974. Four years later she married Raymond, already a Burnham resident, and now the Elstons live behind and over the shop.

Raymond's architectural design studio is at the far end of the house in a converted barn. And Sue's kitchen-cum-dining-room backs on to the shop, serving not only as a thoroughfare for the studio, but also as an information exchange. Throughout the day, a succession of visitors poke their heads through one or other of the kitchen's doorways. Gae Stubbings, who runs the vegetable shop next door, has just been to France and comes in to give Sue a cool-box stuffed with cheeses to sell in the shop.

'Small shopkeepers know who sells what,' Sue explains, 'and so you don't step on one another's toes. Our business is naturally weekend- and holiday-geared. I look for good local cooks to make preserves and do the baking.'

Sue has friends coming for dinner, and when the Elstons have a dinner party, the Heffers are more than likely to be among the guests. Julia arrives early to deliver a batch of baking for the deli' and lend a hand with the preparations.

While Sue has professional experience ('cooking in a local restaurant – nothing grand'), Julia is an inspired natural cook who manages to prepare dishes for the shop when she is not working at her silversmithing partnership in Cambridge. She lives a few miles down the road at Burnham Overy Staithe with her actor husband Richard, and their children.

Julia learnt how to cook from her mother. 'And from Elizabeth David's books, of course. And my stepmother is a wonderful cook – very patient. She can cook anyone under the table. Cooking gives me the same buzz as silversmithing. I love handling the metal, but if you make something disastrous it's rather permanent, whereas with cooking it just gets eaten.'

The two friends decide what to cook. After a busy working day, dinner-party recipes have to be quick and easy. Their normal style of entertaining is informal and relaxed. The menu is settled: potted cockles, courgettes with basil, roasted pepper salad and Norfolk shellfish chowder make up the starters, with olive bread to mop up the juices; Norfolk fish platter with samphire and green sauce, served with baked fennel, is the main dish. To finish, guests will have a choice of Périgord walnut tart or cœur à la crème with summer fruit.

Courgettes with Basil

Serve this as part of a mixed starter with Potted Cockles (see below) and
Roasted Pepper Salad (see page 62).

Serves 6–8 as part of a mixed starter

450 g (1 lb) courgettes
15 ml (1 tbsp) olive oil
15 g (½ oz) butter
1 garlic clove, skinned and chopped

salt and pepper
handful of basil leaves, torn into
   small pieces

Slice the courgettes on the diagonal. Heat the olive oil and butter in a
small saucepan. Add the garlic, then the sliced courgettes. Let them
cook over quite a high heat for a couple of minutes, until they soften a little.

Season with salt and pepper, sprinkle with basil shreds and leave the
salad to cool down to room temperature. Put a spoonful on each plate to
serve.

Potted Cockles

Serve these easy little treats with Courgettes with Basil (see above) and
Roasted Pepper Salad (see page 62).

Serves 6–8 as part of a mixed starter

350 g (12 oz) cockles
juice of ½ lemon
zest of 2 lemons
15 ml (1 tbsp) chopped fennel
   fronds and/or dill

pinch of cayenne
175 g (6 oz) clarified butter, melted

Marinate the cockles in the lemon juice for an hour. Drain the cockles
and toss them with the lemon zest, fennel and cayenne. Pack the
mixture into small moulds, pressing well down. Cover with melted clarified
butter and leave to set. Decant each cockle-castle on to a plate and flank
with the two salads.

Roasted Pepper Salad

Roasted peppers are Sue's current favourites. She usually manages to find a niche for them somewhere on the menu – they look particularly pretty with bright green courgettes.

Serves 6–8 as part of a mixed starter

450 g (1 lb) red peppers
90 ml (6 tbsp) olive oil vinaigrette
a few basil leaves, torn into small
   pieces
225 g (8 oz) sugar peas

3–4 spring onions, trimmed and
   sliced
assorted salad leaves
salt and pepper

Cut round the stalks and squash the peppers flat with the palm of your hand. Grill them until they blister black.

Pop the peppers into a plastic bag for 5 minutes and tie the bag up so that they sweat, making it easier to skin them. Skin, remove the seeds, shred and dress the peppers with vinaigrette and a little fresh basil.

Blanch the sugar peas by throwing them into boiling salted water and draining them as soon as they come back to the boil. Let them cool, then toss them with the sliced spring onions and a selection of salad leaves.

Mix everything together, taste and add salt and pepper. Arrange the salad in small heaps on individual plates.

Olive Bread

This bread has a Mediterranean flavour. The salt gives the olive oil something to kick against. If you add the optional olives, reduce the amount of salt to 10 ml (2 tsp).

Makes 1 huge loaf

900 g (2 lb) strong bread flour
15 ml (1 tbsp) sea salt, crushed
600 ml (1 pint) warm water
50 g (2 oz) fresh yeast

pinch of sugar (optional)
60 ml (4 tbsp) olive oil
50 g (2 oz) black or green olives,
   stoned and chopped (optional)

Sift the flour and the salt into a bowl. Mix half the water with the yeast – you can add a pinch of sugar to get the cells working and frothing.

Make a well in the flour and pour in the yeast mixture. Work the flour and yeast mixture together, adding more warm water, until you have a sticky dough. Knead it for 20 minutes – you can do this in the food processor. Shape it into a soft cushion, then put the dough back in the bowl under a cloth. Leave it to rise for 1½ hours in a warm place; it will need quite a long time because of all the salt.

When the dough has risen, knock it back, and work in the olive oil and the olives, if using. You may need extra flour to take up some of the oil. Form the dough into a neat cushion again, and put it on an oiled and floured baking tray. Let it prove again for 45–60 minutes until it has doubled its bulk. Bake in the oven at 200°C (400°F) mark 6 for 35–45 minutes until well risen and beautifully brown. When it's done it will sound hollow when you tap the base.

Norfolk Shellfish Chowder

You can make this with one or any combination of shellfish: prawns, shrimps – even lobster. Use whatever is fresh and whatever you can afford.

Serves 6–8

900 g (2 lb) mixed shellfish in the shell (clams, cockles, mussels)
8 oysters
900 ml (1½ pints) shellfish liquor, water and white wine together (see method)
small knob of butter
1–2 rashers bacon, chopped

1 medium onion, skinned and chopped
225 g (8 oz) tomatoes, skinned and chopped
1 medium potato, peeled and diced small
150 ml (¼ pint) double cream
salt and pepper

Put the shellfish and oysters to open in a covered pan with a little water over a medium heat. Remove and reserve the shellfish meat and strain the liquor through a sieve lined with a square of muslin or cotton.

Make up the shellfish liquor to 900 ml (1½ pints) with water and a dash of white wine.

Melt the butter in a deep saucepan and fry the bacon and onion for a few minutes. Add the liquid, the tomatoes and the potato and bring the mixture to the boil. Simmer for 10–15 minutes until the potato is soft.

Stir in the shucked shellfish. Reheat and stir in the cream. Taste, and add salt and pepper. Serve the chowder straight away with chunks of Olive Bread (see left).

Norfolk Fish Platter with Samphire

This is the sort of party piece you can prepare when you have access to freshly caught seafood. This quantity serves up to 10 people.

Serves up to 10

The fish
1 sea trout, about 1.6 kg (3½ lb)
3 grey mullet, about 275 g (10 oz) each
3 dabs, 100 g (4 oz) each
1.1 litres (2 pints) whelks in the shell

To cook the fish
sprig of tarragon and marjoram
oil and butter
1–2 lemons
salt and pepper
splash of white wine

For the green sauce
2 good handfuls greens – chard leaves, spinach, watercress, wild goosefoot
300 ml (½ pint) sunflower oil
300 ml (½ pint) olive oil
3 egg yolks
1 egg white
30–45 ml (2–3 tbsp) cider vinegar
handful of chives

To finish
900 g (2 lb) samphire
quartered lemons
vinegar or a vinaigrette for the whelks

Make the green sauce: pick over and rinse the greens. Sweat them briefly over a high heat in a covered saucepan in just the water that clings to the leaves. Leave to cool. Make a mayonnaise in the blender by slowly trickling the oils on to the egg yolks, egg white, and vinegar while the machine is running. Add the cooled blanched leaves and the chives, then season.

Prepare the samphire. Rinse the green twiglets in at least three to four changes of water. Throw the samphire, untrimmed, into a saucepan of boiling water: bring the water back to the boil and simmer for 5 minutes.

Drain and leave until cool enough to handle. Pinch off the pale base of the samphire, pulling out the little woody core as you do so.

Prepare the fish. Lay the sea trout on a square of foil, tuck a sprig of tarragon in the cavity of the sea trout then rub it with oil and dot with butter. Season with salt and pepper and a squeeze of lemon. Wrap the foil and cook the fish in the oven at 200°C (400°F) mark 6 for 35 minutes. The flesh should be firm and springy.

Wipe the mullet. Put a small knob of butter and a sliver of lemon in each cavity. Put each fish on a square of foil. Dot with a little more butter and a few more slivers of lemon. Dribble with white wine. Wrap up the foil and cook in the oven for 10 minutes.

Sprinkle the dabs with marjoram, salt and pepper. Fry them in a little butter and olive oil for 2–3 minutes each side. Although the whelks will have been ready cooked, you'll need to hook each one out of its shell with a pin and pinch off the black curl of cloaca and long black thread of intestine. Slip the whelk neatly back into its shell. Arrange all the fish on a bed of samphire. Serve with quartered lemons and vinegar or vinaigrette for the whelks.

Baked Fennel

Serves 6–8

3–4 bulbs of fennel with their green
   fronds
juice of ½ lemon

60 ml (4 tbsp) olive oil
salt and pepper

Wipe and trim the fennel, saving the green fronds for chopping. Quarter the fennel bulbs and overlap them in a shallow gratin dish. Sprinkle with chopped green fronds. Trickle the lemon juice and oil over the top and season with salt and pepper.

Bake in the oven at 230°C (450°F) mark 8 for 20 minutes until nicely gilded on top – the fennel should still be crisp. Let the fennel cool a little; serve at room temperature.

Cœur à la Crème with Summer Fruit

This summer favourite can be whipped up in no time. Traditionally the dish is made in pierced heart-shaped moulds, hence its name.

Serves 6–8

For the cœur à la crème
225 g (8 oz) cream cheese
150 ml (¼ pint) double cream, whipped stiff
30 ml (2 tbsp) caster sugar
2 egg whites, whisked stiff

For the summer fruit
450 g (1 lb) strawberries
450 g (1 lb) raspberries
225 g (8 oz) cherries
icing sugar to frost the fruit

B eat the cream cheese with the cream and caster sugar. Fold in the egg whites. Tip the mixture into a muslin-lined sieve balanced over a bowl, and leave it overnight. If you leave it for less time, it will be lighter and wobblier, but still delicious.

Hull the fruit and pile it in a pretty glass bowl. Sift icing sugar over the top.

Périgord Walnut Tart

This deliciously chewy tart (which can be made with hazelnuts or almonds, too) is Julia's speciality.

Serves 6–8

For the pastry
175 g (6 oz) butter
225 g (8 oz) plain flour
50 g (2 oz) sugar
1 whole egg, beaten

For the filling
100 g (4 oz) walnuts chopped or ground (not too thoroughly, or the nuts go oily)

75 g (3 oz) granulated sugar
1 egg white, beaten stiff
300 ml (½ pint) double cream, half-whipped

To finish
175 g (6 oz) icing sugar
15 ml (1 tbsp) brandy
12–13 walnut halves, to decorate

Make the pastry by rubbing the butter into the flour and sugar, and working in enough egg to give a light, firm dough. Roll it out into a large enough round to fill a 23 cm (9 inch) tart tin. Bake blind in the oven at 200°C (400°F) mark 6 for 5 minutes.

Mix the filling ingredients together and spread the mixture in the pastry case. Bake for another 30 minutes until the filling is set and the pastry crisp.

Leave to cool. Finish with a layer of icing made by mixing the icing sugar with the brandy and enough water to give the consistency of double cream. Decorate with walnut halves.

Return to Andalucía

Revisiting Andalucía in southern Spain nearly 30 years after I first went there, I found that the pace of life still remains slow. In spite of the much-trumpeted modernity of Seville's Expo '92, the inhabitants still choose their own rhythm, seeing little point in doing today what mañana may render unnecessary.

Cooks in Andalucía have always been happy to gather their ingredients and ideas from anyone and everywhere. Phoenicians and Romans, Celts and Moors have all passed this way, leaving their thumbprints on the pans, their spices in the larder.

So it comes as no surprise to find that José-Maria Gonzalez and Bill Job of the much esteemed La Posada in the little village of Gualchos are not Andalucían born and bred, but inspired incomers.

Their restaurant-hotel is a pair of converted village houses occupying one corner of the little main square, with the life of the village going on all around. Perched high in the Alpujarras, a rugged mountain area with little tourism, Gualchos shelters an independent-minded agricultural community.

Much as the Moors before him, José-Maria wields a sophisticated wooden spoon, marrying fine local ingredients with traditional recipes adapted for educated modern palates, with added inspiration from a lifetime of gastronomic experience all over the world. And it's not hard to spot the foreign influences. The history of the people can even be traced in the crops: Moorish almonds, Roman olives, New World prickly pears and Celtic wheat.

The narrow streets of the old cathedral quarter are lined with the makeshift stalls of the country people, the campesinos, who come daily to sell their produce. The spice-seller's shop, the Andaluz housewife's favourite store, is open to the street in the Moorish fashion, displaying little boxes of precious saffron, cloves and cardamom, cinnamon and pepper and all the spices of Arabia, casks of salt and herrings packed in glistening cartwheels, green lentils, white beans, creamy-yellow chickpeas, rosy cloves of garlic.

But it is for their sweet pastries – ladies' treats – that the invaders from Africa are best remembered. After the Moors left, these sugary pleasures became the province of Christian nuns who marked saints' days and the festivals of the Virgin with special pastries and sweet breads. The Moors loved sherbets and ice-cooled drinks. Snow from the high peaks froze the fruit juices and nut-milks – recipes which can still be enjoyed in the ice-cream parlours of Andalucía's modern cities. José-Maria follows these traditions in his own kitchen, serving delectable desserts, including a delicate saffron-flavoured ice-cream served with spiced wine-poached pears.

La Posada's airy kitchen leads directly into the deliciously shady garden, overlooking tumbling red roofs trawled by flights of swifts. The hills beyond are carpeted with wild rosemary and thyme, sage and oregano, lavender and the feathery fronds of wild fennel.

Does it sound like the garden of Eden? It is. Here's what's cooking in paradise.

Golden Rice in Seafood Sauce

There are rice paddies up and down the Andalucían littoral, although the most famous are those of Valencia. This dish differs from a paella, defined by the double-handled dish in which all the ingredients cook, in that the rice and fish are cooked and served in separate pans.

Serves 4–6

For the rice
45 ml (3 tbsp) olive oil
4 garlic cloves, skinned and
   chopped
550 g (1¼ lb) round (pudding) rice
700 g (1½ lb) tomatoes, skinned,
   deseeded and chopped
2.5 ml (½ tsp) saffron threads,
   soaked in a splash of boiling
   water
salt and pepper
1.5 litres (2½ pints) fish stock
   (made with fish-heads and
   bones, plenty of aromatics and
   white wine)

For the prawns and the sauce
450–550 g (1–1¼ lb) fresh unpeeled
   prawns
olive oil
3 garlic cloves, unpeeled and
   roughly chopped
1 glass brandy
1 small glass white wine
1 medium onion, skinned and finely
   chopped
1 small green pepper, deseeded and
   cubed small
1 small red pepper, deseeded and
   cubed small
30 ml (2 tbsp) olive oil
2 tomatoes, skinned, deseeded and
   chopped

Warm the oil in a wide shallow pan. Throw in the garlic and let it soften for a moment. Add the rice to the pan and stir it briefly until it becomes transparent.

Stir in the tomatoes and saffron with its water, and turn up the heat a little. When it bubbles up, season with salt and pepper and add the hot fish stock gradually, during 15–18 minutes of cooking (as you would for a risotto).

By that time, all the liquid should be used up, and the rice should be juicy and still slightly *al dente*. Let it rest for 10 minutes. Meanwhile, make the sauce for the prawns.

Peel the prawns and reserve the flesh. Put all the debris into a frying pan with a slick of olive oil and the roughly chopped garlic cloves. Sauté everything gently together until the prawn shells are light brown. Add the brandy and the wine, and bubble everything up for 5–10 minutes to evaporate the alcohol and concentrate the juices. Tip the contents of the pan into a blender and process them thoroughly. Sieve thoroughly, reserving the liquid.

Meanwhile, sauté the onion and peppers gently in 30 ml (2 tbsp) olive oil, add the tomatoes and bubble everything up again. Add the prawn liquid and reheat to boiling. Season. Add the raw prawns and let them turn opaque in the hot sauce. Serve the prawns with the rice.

Almond Soup

Thickening soups and sauces with bread is common in the cookery of Andalucía – perhaps it comes naturally to those the Romans nominated the best bakers in their empire.

Serves 4

90 ml (6 tbsp) olive oil
225 g (8 oz) blanched almonds
2 slices day-old bread, cubed
2 garlic cloves, skinned and
   roughly chopped
2–3 parsley sprigs, roughly
   chopped

5 ml (1 tsp) cumin seeds
6–8 saffron threads
750 ml (1¼ pints) water
salt and pepper

To serve
garlic croûtons
slivered toasted almonds

Heat the olive oil in a small frying pan. Add the almonds, half the bread, the garlic and parsley, and brown gently. Either pound the mixture to a paste with the cumin and the saffron in a pestle and mortar, or tip the contents of the pan, plus the cumin and saffron, into a food processor and process it with a little water to a smooth paste.

Transfer the paste to a saucepan and stir in the water. Bring gently to the boil, turn down the heat and simmer for 5 minutes. Remove it from the heat and stir in the remaining bread cubes. Cover and leave for 10 minutes to allow the bread to go spongy. Season to taste. Serve with croûtons and slivered toasted almonds.

Salt-Cod Salad

Salt-cod – *bacalao* – was once a useful meat substitute for the peoples of the Mediterranean, who observed the strict abstinence days of the Roman Catholic church. The taste for this Atlantic-caught delicacy, now an expensive luxury, has lingered long after the weekly religious obligation has been lifted.

Serves 4

200 g (7 oz) bacalao, soaked for 48 hours (or use raw smoked haddock instead)

1 green pepper, deseeded and finely sliced

1 red pepper, deseeded and finely sliced

2–3 beef tomatoes, deseeded and cubed

1 large Spanish onion, skinned and cut into slivers

15 ml (1 tbsp) chopped fresh parsley

1–2 garlic cloves, skinned and chopped

75 g (3 oz) black and green olives, stoned and sliced

45 ml (3 tbsp) olive oil

15 ml (1 tbsp) lemon juice

salt and cayenne pepper

1 hard-boiled egg, chopped (optional)

To serve
bread
lettuce leaves

With your fingers, remove the skin and the bones from the fish. Flake the flesh. Toss all the ingredients, except the lettuce leaves, together in a bowl. You won't need any salt – the fish is salty anyway. You can include chopped hard-boiled egg if you like: optional but traditional.

Serve cool, with bread and crisp lettuce leaves to scoop up the dressing.

Stuffed Artichokes

Granada is famous for its artichokes, cousins of the native thistle. These kingly plants were first cultivated in the *vega*, Granada's garden-plateau, where the Moors perfected the irrigation system installed by the Romans. Serve this dish as part of a selection of mixed appetisers or as a light and summery first course or lunch dish.

Serves 4

4 large or 8 small artichokes

For the stuffing
450 g (1 lb) spinach, blanched, drained and finely chopped
100 g (4 oz) jamón serrano (or Parma ham, lean bacon or gammon), finely chopped
2 anchovy fillets, chopped
225 g (8 oz) mushrooms, finely chopped
1 ogg

For the sauce
45 ml (3 tbsp) olive oil
1 small carrot, finely chopped
1 small onion, skinned and finely chopped
1 garlic clove, skinned and chopped
1 thyme sprig
1 bay leaf
salt and pepper

To finish
1 glass dry white wine and 1 glass water

Trim the hard outer leaves from the artichokes. Trim the inner leaves so that most of what is left is tender enough to eat. With a sharp knife, nick out the hairy choke.

Combine all the stuffing ingredients and form the mixture into four or eight balls. Pop these into the space left by the removal of the choke.

Make the sauce: heat the oil in a heavy wide pan. Add the sauce vegetables, garlic and herbs and cook until soft. Season. Set the stuffed artichokes to stew gently in the sauce, covered with a tight-fitting lid, for 20–30 minutes.

Test the artichokes' bases with a darning needle. When they are nearly tender, pour in a glass of dry white wine and a glass of water. Cover again and continue cooking for a further 10–15 minutes.

Take out the artichokes. Boil the liquid rapidly to reduce it, then adjust the seasoning. Pour the finished sauce round the artichokes.

Fish Balls

This is José-Maria's adaptation of the standard Monday dish of the Andaluz housewife.

Serves 4

1 large egg
1 garlic clove, skinned
1 large parsley sprig
2 large spring onions
5 ml (1 tsp) capers

salt and 2.5 ml (1/2 tsp) cayenne
  pepper
225 g (8 oz) raw fresh fish, skinned
  and deboned
oil for frying
lemon juice

Put all the ingredients except the oil and lemon juice in a food processor, adding the fish last, and give them a good pounding. Wet your hands and form the paste into little balls, each about the size of a small egg.

Heat the oil in a pan (a heavy-based, cast-iron pan is best). Fry the little balls until they are golden, drain on absorbent kitchen paper and serve piping hot with a good squeeze of lemon juice.

Quails with Raisins and Malaga Wine

Extravagant but delicious.

Serves 4

handful of raisins
150 ml (1/4 pint) brandy mixed with
  water
8 quails
15 ml (1 tbsp) olive oil

Malaga wine
15 ml (1 tbsp) lemon juice
25 g (1 oz) butter
25 g (1 oz) arrowroot
2–3 thyme sprigs

Soak the raisins in the brandy and water for 2 hours. Remove the raisins from the marinade and reserve both.

Brown the quails in the oil and deglaze with the marinade and a glass of Malaga wine. Add the raisins. Cook for 30 minutes over a gentle heat. Add the lemon juice.

Remove the quails and keep warm. Mix together the butter, arrowroot and a dash of Malaga wine and stir into the cooking liquor. Heat, stirring, until thickened. Pour over the quail and serve garnished with thyme.

Pears in Wine with Saffron Ice-Cream

This is a lovely combination – deep burgundy-coloured pears and pale yellow ice-cream. The delicate flavour of the fruit perfectly complements the subtle, dusty flavour of the saffron.

Serves 4–6

For the ice-cream
300 ml (½ pint) milk
5 ml (1 tsp) saffron threads
4 egg yolks
60 ml (4 tbsp) sugar
300 ml (½ pint) double cream

For the pears
4–8 firm but ripe pears (size dictates quantity)

1 bottle full-bodied Spanish red wine
5 cm (2 inch) cinnamon stick
2 cloves
8 peppercorns
1 bay leaf
175 g (6 oz) sugar
juice of 1 lemon

First make the ice-cream. Boil the milk with the saffron. Remove from the heat. Put the egg yolks and sugar into a bowl and gradually whisk in the saffron milk. Then set the bowl over a saucepan of simmering water and whisk it until it thickens to a custardy consistency.

Let the mixture cool and whisk in the cream. Freeze the ice-cream in the usual way. If you use the ice-making compartment of the refrigerator, take out the ice-cream when it is nearly solid and beat it thoroughly. This is hard work.

Peel the pears and arrange them in a heavy saucepan just large enough to accommodate them. Mix together the rest of the ingredients, and pour them over the pears.

Bring everything to the boil, turn down the heat, cover and let the pears poach gently for 30–40 minutes until tender.

Remove the fruit and reserve. Turn up the heat and boil the liquid fiercely, uncovered, until it reduces by half. Remove the ice-cream from the freezer to allow it to soften it a little. Arrange pears in a bowl, strain syrup and pour it around the pears. Serve with the ice-cream.

Summer in Ireland

Tucked into the green foothills of the Mountains of Mourne, along the coast from County Down's seaside resort of Newcastle, lie Glassdrumman House and its home farm. The hotel and its newly dug garden are protected from the winds and passing cows by a handsome new stone wall made in the old way – using the enormous smooth round boulders that litter the fields as if a giant's child had grown bored with a game of marbles.

Proprietors Joan and Graeme Hall came here 10 years ago. 'We bought it, along with 60 acres, and opened a farm shop for the first three or four years, to sell our surplus. And then somehow it spread out – first a coffee shop, then a restaurant. And now the hotel.'

Graeme, a town-bred Yorkshireman, is more at home on the kitchen range than on the prairie. 'Farming is fine as a life-style,' he says, 'but cooking is a necessity. We realised we had to be able to rely on good raw ingredients – that's why we started farming.'

The Halls have founded a community at Glassdrumman: Baptist-based and born-again Christian, but unlabelled so that all denominations can feel welcome. It now numbers some 40 people, as well as the Jersey cows, the Aberdeen Angus bull, the horse, three ponies, and a handful of goats and breeding sows.

Graeme did all the cooking at first but has now turned his saucepans over to his talented young apprentice, Steve Webb.

Dryad's saddle fungi grow outside the kitchen window; sea-beet is gathered on the shore to be made into a soup, and packed into a hamper for guests to have an alfresco supper at the opera at nearby Castle Ward.

From hand-churned butter and fresh eggs to delicate salad leaves and edible flowers, the enterprise is underpinned by the farm. Nicky Brown, the farm manager, was born to the land. His grandfather farmed 250 acres across the border in County Monaghan.

Nicky has no illusions about organic farming: 'We made a few mistakes at the beginning. We had no idea how long it would take to support ourselves or how far back you need to go in the food chain before you can become organic. We de-stocked to fund the work on the hotel, but we're building the farming up again and trying to get it right this time.' The vegetables are all grown organically and the cattle aren't pumped full of hormones.

The farm extends to 120 acres, half owned outright and the other half rented, and most of it is pasture. 'Ireland's greatest natural resource is grass,' Nicky explains. 'Here you need one acre per animal: we concentrate on Aberdeen Angus crossed with the Dairy Shorthorn – which gives a blue-grey, an old breed popular in Ireland. I can take you down the road and show you my breeding stock in every local farmer's field.'

The pace of rural Ireland remains as gentle as the weather. Joan, responding to the beauty of St Patrick's beloved mountains, reckons she has come home: 'Graeme gets bored and wants to be off and doing new things. But it's wonderful for the children to be able to grow up in this beautiful place.'

Fish Bisque with Prawns and Mussels

Restaurant chefs always have access to marvellous trimmings for their soups. Steve's fish stockpot contains an exotic mixture of monkfish and salmon bones, oyster and mussel shells and liquor, lobster carapace and heads, and prawn debris. If you are making the fish terrine (see page 80), the trimmings should yield enough extra stock for this soup – particularly if you supplement it with extra bones and fishheads from your fishmonger.

Serves 4

25 g (1 oz) butter	600 ml (1 pint) fish stock
1 onion, skinned and chopped	150 ml (1/4 pint) double cream
1–2 carrots, sliced	50 g (2 oz) cooked, shelled mussels
1–2 sticks of fennel or celery, sliced	50 g (2 oz) peeled prawns
a few parsley stalks	
1 tomato, chopped (could be the	To finish
leftover bits from the terrine)	crisply fried croûtons
5–6 saffron threads	lemon slices
1 glass white wine	

In a large saucepan, melt the butter and sweat the onion, carrots and fennel or celery until they are soft but not coloured. Add the parsley, chopped tomato and saffron and turn up the heat.

Add the white wine and let it bubble up. Reduce until you get a thick butter–wine emulsion. Pour in the stock, bring to the boil and turn down the heat. Let the soup simmer for 10 minutes.

Remove from the heat, skim and stir in the cream. Reheat gently to just below boiling.

Divide the mussels and prawns between the plates. Pour in the soup. Garnish with croûtons and lemon slices.

FISH STOCK

Make fish stock with all available trimmings. Start it in cold water and reinforce with vegetable trimmings (don't use anything from the cabbage family). Simmer for 30 minutes, then strain.

Beet and Broccoli Soup

The Irish weather being a little unreliable even in high summer, a hot soup can be very welcome on a picnic. The sea-beet Steve uses grows wild round the shores of Britain: collect it at this time of year from a clean dune. Sometimes it is salty, sometimes as bland as chard leaves. To add extra flavour to the soup, Steve used the trimmings from the broccoli in the fish terrine.

Serves 4

225 g (8 oz) trimmed sea-beet (or chard leaves, spinach or lettuce)
25 g (1 oz) butter
2 medium onions or 1 Spanish onion, skinned and finely chopped
1 garlic clove, unpeeled
225 g (8 oz) broccoli trimmings, chopped
150 ml (¼ pint) white wine
900 ml (1½ pints) homemade stock, strained

1 large potato, peeled and cut into small cubes
salt and pepper
juice of 1 lemon
45–60 ml (3–4 tbsp) cream

To garnish (optional)
a few cooked peeled prawns or mussels (if you are using sea-beet)

Wash and shred the leaves (saving one or two for garnishing). Melt the butter in a large saucepan and add the onion and the whole unpeeled garlic clove. Let them sweat gently in the butter for 5–6 minutes. Stir in the shredded leaves and broccoli. Let the vegetables soften over a low heat. Pour in the white wine and let everything bubble up and cook down.

Remove the garlic, then pour in the stock and bring to the boil. Add the potato and simmer for about 15 minutes. Purée the soup and then sieve it. Taste and add salt and pepper, and enough lemon juice to sharpen the flavour. Reheat and finish with a little cream and the shredded leaves. Garnish with prawns or mussels, if wished.

Dryad's Saddle in Brandy

Wild fungi (and mature cultivated mushrooms) benefit from a quick flame with alcohol: the brief roasting accentuates the woody flavour.

Serves 2 as a starter

1–2 tender dryad's saddle fungi or
    225 g (8 oz) large cultivated
    mushrooms
25 g (1 oz) butter
1 small onion, skinned and finely
    chopped

15 ml (1 tbsp) brandy
small glass white wine
salt and pepper

Slice the fungi and fry with the butter and onion until all the liquid has evaporated. Add the brandy and set it alight. Add the white wine and let it all reduce to a shiny emulsion. Season with a little salt and a sprinkle of pepper.

Fish Terrine with Saffron Aspic

The ingredients for this lovely pink and green terrine are assembled when cooked, rather than baked together. Steve serves it with a sauce of avocado puréed with a splash of the fish stock.

Makes 12 slices

450 g (1 lb) smoked or dilled
    salmon
450 g (1 lb) monkfish on the bone
450 g (1 lb) unshelled scampi
    (Dublin Bay prawns)
600 ml (1 pint) fish stock
6–8 saffron threads
25 g (1 oz) powdered gelatine

15 g (½ oz) butter
5 ml (1 tsp) chopped onion
350 g (12 oz) broccoli
salt
350 g (12 oz) tomatoes
30 ml (2 tbsp) finely chopped fresh
    parsley

Line a terrine or long loaf tin with salmon or gravlax slices (not at either end, though, that would be a waste). Lay the slices up the sides, so that there are long flaps left to be folded over to enclose the terrine.

Bone the monkfish and slice the fillets thinly. Peel the scampi. Salt the monkfish lightly.

In a saucepan, bring a ladleful of the fish stock to the boil with the saffron. Put in the monkfish slices and let them poach for 3–4 minutes, until cooked through. Remove the fish and put It aside to cool.

Add the rest of the fish stock to the saffron stock in the pan, mix in the gelatine, and stir it over the heat until all the granules dissolve. Sieve it, pressing to extract all the colour from the saffron (or, for a good strong colour, put it all in a food processor), and set it aside to cool. How much of the aspic you use depends on how tightly the layers are packed – the gelatine is used at twice the usual strength because the terrine juices will dilute it.

Fry the scampi briefly in a scrap of butter with the onion. Divide the broccoli tops into florets. Peel and quarter the stalks lengthways. Drop them in a pan of boiling salted water and simmer for 5–6 minutes until tender. Drain well and cool. Scald, skin, deseed and finely chop the tomatoes.

Assemble the terrine. Pour in the cool saffron aspic as you go, layer by layer. The cooler the ingredients the less moisture they exude and the better the set. First layer in half the monkfish, then the parsley, followed by the scampi, the broccoli, the rest of the monkfish and finally the tomato. Fold over the flaps of salmon to enclose the terrine. Chill in the refrigerator for 2–3 hours; remove and leave to set overnight.

GLASSDRUMMAN'S OPERA HAMPER

Castle Ward is a National Trust property on the south shore of Strangford Lough, about 40 minutes' drive from Glassdrumman. Its short opera season is very popular. As at Glyndebourne, the audience wears black tie and long dresses, and the food from the hampers is served in the pink-and-white marquee in the interval. For a night at the opera, Steve's hamper for-four people might contain Beet and Broccoli Soup, Fish Terrine with Saffron Aspic, Turkey Breast with Peppers, Marinated Fillet of Beef and a salad.

Cheese Bread

This rich, golden bread is simple to make and is ideal for picnics, or to serve with a bowl of soup or a light evening meal – along with a glass of red wine. One of Steve's favourite bread recipes, he admits he got it from his mum!

Makes 1 loaf

15 g (½ oz) fresh yeast
5 ml (1 tsp) sugar
150 ml (¼ pint) warm milk
250 g (9 oz) flour

50 g (2 oz) unsalted butter, melted
2.5 ml (½ tsp) salt
75 g (3 oz) Cheddar cheese, grated
beaten egg, to glaze

Cream the yeast with the sugar and a little milk. Put the flour in a bowl, making a well in the centre. Pour in the yeast mixture, the rest of the milk, the butter and the salt. Mix to a smooth dough, knead for 10 minutes, then cover with a damp cloth and leave for 1 hour.

Knock back and divide into 24 small balls. Place them in layers of eight in a greased bread tin, and cover each layer – except the top one – with grated cheese, reserving a little for the top.

Prove for 1 hour, brush with beaten egg and bake in the oven at 220°C (425°F) mark 7 for 30–45 minutes. Sprinkle on more grated cheese 10 minutes before the loaf is cooked.

Turkey Breast with Peppers

This is not just pretty picnic food; Steve maintains that the peppers give the bland turkey meat a piquant flavour. Remember to slice the peppers into ribbons lengthways: if you do them in the usual way as rings they will be too curved to slide in easily.

Serves 4

1 turkey breast, weighing about
   350 g (12 oz)
3 ribbons of red pepper and 3 of
   green

salt and pepper
25 g (1 oz) butter

Skin the turkey breast and lay it what would have been skin-side down on the table. With a slender sharp knife, make a long diagonal stab in the turkey breast, going with the grain of the meat. Lift the knife to make a space beneath and slip in a ribbon of pepper. Repeat five times.

Sprinkle with salt and pepper and dot with butter and wrap it in foil, folding with a double pleat on top and closing the ends to seal in the juices. Bake in the oven at 200°C (400°F) mark 6 for 45 minutes. Let the turkey cool before you unwrap it. Turn it over to slice it.

Marinated Fillet of Beef

This simple recipe underlines the fine flavour of the beef from Glassdrumman's own herd. Make sure the meat is well-trimmed or it will shrink out of shape.

Serves 4

450 g (1 lb) fillet steak in a single
  piece
15 ml (1 tbsp) olive oil
1 garlic clove, skinned and crushed
15 ml (1 tbsp) chopped fresh
  rosemary
15 ml (1 tbsp) chopped fresh basil
15 ml (1 tbsp) chopped fresh
  parsley

5 ml (1 tsp) fresh thyme
5 ml (1 tsp) freshly ground pepper

To serve
horseradish grated into a little
  whipped cream

Make six lengthways cuts 1 cm (½ inch) deep all round the fillet. Work the oil and all the aromatics into a paste and rub it into the meat, pushing it well into the cuts. Leave to marinate overnight.

The next day, roast the meat in the oven at 200°C (400°F) mark 6 for 15–20 minutes, when it will still be pink. Let it cool, then slice it. Serve with horseradish grated into a little whipped cream.

A Devon Teatime

Up the hill beyond the picturesque medieval stannary town of Chagford, past the old tin mines tucked away between the folds of valley that edge the tor-strewn wilderness of Dartmoor, is Higher Murchington Farm – home to four generations of the dairy-farming Vincents.

The high moors of Devon do not easily yield their secrets. Thick hedgerows, riotous with wild flowers in early summer, veil sloping green pastures and thatch-roofed farmhouses dwarfed by their steadings. Six-foot-high drystone walls ribbon the valleys. Blind corners and unexplained crossroads afford sudden glimpses of ruminating cows. The thousands of summer tourists who crowd the narrow deep-cut lanes might easily pass on their way without a glance at the small farms, such as Higher Murchington, which provide local tea shops with clotted cream and their new venture, dairy ices made with real fruit.

Great-grandmother Connie Vincent lives in a cottage just up the hill from the old house. When she first arrived 34 years ago, there was an apple orchard and kitchen garden to keep the household supplied with cider and vegetables, together with a few rows of anemones for a small cash crop.

Connie is the star cook of the family. Everyone comes up the hill for Nan Connie's Sunday roast of home-reared pork with all the trimmings, cooked to perfection in the ever-glowing Rayburn.

Down the lane from Connie's cottage is the new bungalow which her son Ken and his wife Lyn have just moved into after more than three decades of farming Higher Murchington's 130 acres, to make way for the next generation of farming Vincents in the farmhouse itself. Lyn's family, the Leamans, have been in Chagford for 700 years – they were masons and carpenters by trade. Ken and Lyn have just turned the farm over to son Duncan and his wife Robyn, with help from Duncan's brother Ian.

When your day starts with milking at 6.30 am and you're still working at 8 o'clock in the evening, tea is one of the main pleasures of the day – a fine old-fashioned Devonshire cream tea, with everything, from the raspberry jam to the strong, rough, draught cider, the cookies to the ice-cream, made on the farm.

Fruit Buns

Ken Vincent likes these as his harvest tea, made as thick as a man's fist, spread with clotted cream, and washed down with rough cider.

Makes 10–12

225 g (8 oz) self-raising flour
1.25 ml (¼ tsp) salt
75 g (3 oz) butter or lard
75 g (3 oz) sugar

100 g (4 oz) raisins and sultanas
 (mixed peel too, if you like it)
1 egg
150 ml (¼ pint) milk

Sift the flour and salt into a bowl. Rub in the butter or lard. Stir in the sugar and fruit. Whisk the egg and milk together and stir in enough to make a mixture which drops easily from the spoon.

Drop spoonfuls into a well-buttered bun tray. Bake in the oven at 200°C (400°F) mark 6 for 15–20 minutes.

Raspberry Buns with Cream

These buns are perfect for a summer picnic. Clotted cream is the essential accompaniment.

Makes 10–12

225 g (8 oz) self-raising flour
100 g (4 oz) butter
100 g (4 oz) caster sugar
1 egg yolk

about 60 ml (4 tbsp) milk
225 g (8 oz) raspberry jam (or fresh
 raspberries mashed with a little
 sugar)

Sift the flour, rub in the butter and stir in the sugar. Mix in the yolk and enough milk to make a firm pastry for rolling. Roll out and cut out rounds with a pint glass. Put a teaspoon of jam or fresh raspberries in the middle of each round. Moisten the edges with milk and bunch up the pastry to enclose the jam as if making a doughnut. Turn over and brush with milk.

Place in a bun tray, or on a greased baking tray and bake in the oven at 200°C (400°F) mark 6 for 10–15 minutes until well-risen and golden. Serve with thick clotted cream, to spread on like butter.

Creamy Cheesecake

This is the perfect teatime treat – or serve it with ice-cream as a dessert. You can leave out the dried fruits if you prefer, or vary the flavourings. Grated orange rind, cinnamon and a sweetening of honey instead of the sugar is delicious.

Serves 4–6

For the pastry
65 g (2¹/₂ oz) butter
65 g (2¹/₂ oz) lard
200 g (7 oz) plain flour
30–45 ml (2–3 tbsp) ice-cold water

For the filling
350 g (12 oz) cottage cheese

75 g (3 oz) butter, softened
50 g (2 oz) sugar
50 g (2 oz) plain flour
3 egg yolks
300 ml (¹/₂ pint) double cream
50 g (2 oz) sultanas and raisins
grated rind of 1 lemon

Make the pastry by rubbing the butter and lard into the flour, and working in enough cold water to give a light, firm dough. Roll out the pastry on a lightly floured surface and use it to line a deep tart tin.

Sieve the cottage cheese, then work in the softened butter, the sugar and the flour. Beat in the egg yolks and cream. Stir in the sultanas and raisins and the grated lemon rind.

Bake the pastry blind in the oven at 200°C (400°F) mark 6 for 15 minutes, then pour in the filling mixture and bake for another 35 minutes until firm and nicely browned.

Blackcurrant Ice-Cream

Use fresh or frozen berries, or home-made jam sharpened with a squeeze of lemon – in which case omit the sugar.

Makes 1.5 litres (2¹/₂ pints)

300 ml (¹/₂ pint) double cream
300 ml (¹/₂ pint) milk
4 eggs, separated

120 ml (8 tbsp) sugar
450 g (1 lb) blackcurrants

Process the cream and the milk with the egg yolks and sugar in a blender. Pour the mixture into a bowl and set it over a saucepan of simmering water. Whisk until the custard thickens enough to coat the spoon. Leave to cool.

Pick over the blackcurrants and remove any bits of stalk. Process the fruit to a thick purée and stir it into the custard. Freeze for 1–2 hours until the edges are solid but the middle is soft.

Beat the mixture and fold in the stiffly whisked egg whites. Freeze again, until solid. Serve with clotted cream, summer berries and Devon Cookies (see below).

Devon Cookies

These crisp, spicy biscuits are Nan Connie's speciality – they are excellent with home-made ice-cream, or for tea with clotted cream.

Makes 10–12

30 ml (2 tbsp) golden syrup
100 g (4 oz) butter
175 g (6 oz) self-raising flour

5 ml (1 tsp) powdered ginger
1.25 ml (¼ tsp) bicarbonate of soda

Melt the syrup and butter in a small saucepan. Sift together the flour, ginger and bicarbonate of soda. Fold the dry ingredients into the syrup and butter. The mixture should be quite runny and fall off the spoon.

Drop teaspoons of the mixture on to a buttered baking sheet, leaving them plenty of room to spread.

Bake in the oven at 180°C (350°F) mark 4 for 10–15 minutes. If you put them in too hot an oven, they burn at the edges before they are done. Leave them on the baking sheet to firm up for a minute or two. Transfer them to a baking tray to cool and become crisp.

CLOTTED CREAM

Cornish clotted cream is traditionally made by separating the milk before scalding the cream in wide shallow pans. The old Devon way was to scald the milk and skim off the clotted cream – this required plenty of space and a very large battery of scalding pans. Now the Vincents have a large separator to make the clotted cream.

AFTERNOON TEA

Afternoon tea is the meal at which the cooks of our fertile island come into their own. This great achievement of the British kitchen is at its best in the capable hands of a country cook, well-versed in her grandmother's culinary habits, who has access to the best ingredients, including fresh eggs from chickens which have done a bit of their own foraging. This is the perfect showcase for our traditional strengths: baking and dairy products, a larder well-stocked with potted and spiced meats, jam and preserves. No other national cuisine has anything like it.

The French call their own apology for the meal *le five-o'clock*, in homage to its origins. Even so, a madeleine to dip into a pale infusion hardly has the glamour of a double-tiered cake-stand crowded with the best of British baking.

The beverage itself received early attention from Sir Kenelm Digby, necromancer and founder member in 1660 of the Royal Society, who stipulated that the leaves of *cha*, brought back from China by a Jesuit acquaintance, must be left to brew for 'no longer than it takes to say the *Miserere* very leisurely'. In the elegant 18th century, afternoon tea became a delightful piece of theatre for fashionable society ladies – tea-gowns and afternoon-dresses provided a background for beautiful china tea-sets, fine silver, and perhaps a little flirting.

The meal itself was welcomed into the country-house nursery not least by Nanny, who complained that those heavy 10-course Victorian dinners kept the children awake.

Monica Rawlins remembers, as a young woman in the 1920s, presiding over afternoon tea at Syston Park near Bristol. The ritual was, she recalls, quite as important as the refreshment. The teaset – Spode or Minton, Wedgwood or Worcester – would be chosen with a careful eye to the occasion and the visitors expected.

As Monica's father was a widower, it was her privilege to pour the tea – a task which could be performed only by the senior lady of the house. After their mother died, Monica remembers her brothers dashing upstairs to find her when tea was being brought, calling: 'Quick, or so-and-so will pour.'

Tea at Syston was taken in the drawing room. China and Indian tea were both served, and in Monica's mother's day there was always coffee too. A three-layered cake-stand dominated the table. The lowest tier had thin bread and butter, to be spread with jam made at home with fruits from the garden. In winter there might be a dish of crumpets or muffins too. The next layer had little triangular sandwiches – crusts neatly trimmed – filled with tomatoes or cucumber from the greenhouse, potted home-cured ham, or Gentleman's Relish. On the top tier was the cake: a cherry cake, perhaps, or a sponge.

Afternoon tea is the meal at which we feel able to let down our national hair. A friendly, festive, leisurely occasion at which young and old, family and casual guest, can come and go as they please taking a crumb of shortbread here, a nugget of lardy-cake there. It remains a movable feast, a meal to be taken in the freckled shade of the garden among the scents of roses and lavender in our short sweet summers, or cosily by the fire in the long wet winters.

It is, in short, the posy on our culinary bonnet, the stuff of dreams. The poet Rupert Brooke knew well what heady memories he conjured up when he wrote of the meadows of Grantchester. Long indeed may there be honey still for tea.

AUTUMN

Where I now live in deepest rural Wales, everyone is acutely aware of the year's passing. The year's crop of lambs are sent to market, the chickens come off the lay, the cows are brought in and the flavour of the milk reflects the winter fodder.

Winter is on its way, and it's time to think about stocking up the larder. The deep-freeze now swallows up the fruits and vegetables of summer – so we no longer need to salt down the beans or bottle the peas. And it's true that no one needs to make chutney or pickles or jam when we can buy commercially prepared versions, saving time and – most probably – money. Nevertheless, every year, confronted with a glut of apples or plums, a hedgerow full of berries or a crop of green tomatoes, I can't resist pickling and bottling and jellying. In my travels, I'm pleased to find that there are plenty of us out there putting up the preserves, dunking the sloes in the gin, brewing up the ginger beer.

Game is the great autumn treat – St. Hubert's day traditionally marks the start of the hunting season. Lucky countrydwellers can lay their hands on a mixed bag of whatever falls to the local hunters' guns, with shooting for the pot as well as the sport. There's nothing better than a brace of fat pigeons for the stew or a plump little rabbit for a pie. Except perhaps a potted grouse, or a nicely roasted haunch of venison, as dished up by the lady of the castle herself.

Then there's the autumn crop of wild fungi to be gathered – my own repertoire has been greatly expanded by Roger Phillips, mushroom-expert extraordinary, who takes most of the photographs for my articles in Country Living. *My neighbours seem to confine their gathering to field mushrooms, leaving me free range of the woods and* a prolific harvest of chanterelles and ceps to be dried in the airing cupboard for the winter stews and soups. By the way – a hot tip for anyone who lives in a damp house and has a de-humidifier: it's perfect for drying fungi.

Frosty autumn weather calls for comfortable old-fashioned broths – and the Welsh cawl fits the bill. One of that catholic group of soup-stews which includes the French pot-au-feu and the Italian bollito misto, a joint of bacon is the favourite broth-meat and a wooden bowl the supping-dish. For the more adventurous, a plain boiled dinner is lovely spiced up with a little sharp-flavoured sauce – or three.

To round off the meal, bread puddings are the careful housewife's traditional stand-by – particularly if you have been baking your own bread. There's a fine repertoire of these classic desserts, easily assembled and put to cook in the oven at the same time as the roast or hot-pot.

There are domestic chores to be completed: the woodshed to be filled; the garden to be bedded down; autumn leaves to be cleared from gutters. I have a five-foot-long wooden spoon bought in a Hungarian market which now does duty not, as the wood-carver intended, to stir a simmering cauldron of plum jam, but to ladle the leaves out of blocked drainpipes. At this time of year there seem to be endless excuses for stirring something up.

Cook of the Castle

'You can tell the days when Cherry has been busy making jam. The telephone's sticky.' Humphrey Drummond locates the elderly instrument, its amiable tinkle muffled under the papers overflowing the large desk on which his wife, the 16th Baroness Strange of Megginch, has just finished checking a House of Lords briefing on a fact-finding trip. Humphrey has a biography to finish. The computer-fixer in Perth has to be telephoned as the word-processor is playing up.

Cherry herself, with a bundle of files clamped under one arm, has disappeared down the turret staircase into the cavernous depths of Megginch Castle's kitchens to pot up the rest of her redcurrant jelly. Mother of six, hereditary peeress in her own right (there are not many of those about – even in Scotland), she is also an authoress with two romantic novels, a biography and a string of poems under her belt.

Kitchen cupboards overflow with jams, jellies and home-made wines. Cherry has decorated the doors with her sketches of favourite herbs and aromatics.

The jelly neatly potted, Cherry, in her special cherry-appliquéd apron, bustles about making mint tea. She is precise in her recipe: 3 spikes of applemint to 1 of peppermint – and lots of sugar. 'And I'm throwing up scones for tea. All Scots-women "*throw up*" scones. Not too much fat in them or they'll be brittle.'

The castle winds around itself like the trunk of an ancient lightning-struck oak. Visitors can disappear into its passages for days. Even better – so can the owners when under pressure of work. There has been a dwelling here for at least a thousand years: the first four walls were standing in 1460; the stone turret was added in the 16th century, just after the Drummonds acquired the castle, and in 1707 John – Cherry calls him the building Drummond – added the first recorded brickwork in Scotland.

The kitchen garden supplies all the household's vegetables, herbs, flowers and fruit. Specialities include a big bed of chicory, its roots stored indoors and blanched under thick layers of newspaper to give Christmas supplies of crunchy pale leaves. Spinach and Good King Henry, beans and peas, baby marrows, carrots, broad beans and broccoli are all there for the picking.

For the winter, root vegetables are stored in sand, apples and pears in trays, soft fruit and plums are bottled and jammed. The newly rebuilt greenhouse has a fine crop of tomatoes for summer salads and autumn chutney. Against the 18th-century brick double-wall – its hollow heart heated by hot air from the boiler that warms the greenhouse – peaches, apricots and nectarines ripen in the soft east-coast sunshine.

Cherry's new project is an astrological garden, planted as a six-pointed star centred on the sun, each point dedicated to its own heavenly body and containing a selection of the appropriate herbs and flowers.

Potted Grabbit with Whisky

Grabbit – named by Humphrey – is grouse-and-rabbit. The first can be replaced by pigeon or any feathered game, the second with chicken. The recipe is an adaptation of the classic French *terrine de faisan* – the sweet nuts complement the delicate flavour of the game.

Serves 8–10 as a first course

2 grouse, pigeon or partridge or 1 pheasant, plucked
1 wild rabbit, skinned, about 350 g (12 oz)
grated rind of 1 lemon
5 ml (1 tsp) crushed juniper berries
5 ml (1 tsp) each chopped fresh thyme and marjoram
salt and pepper

1 wine glass good red wine or port
30 ml (2 tbsp) whisky
225 g (8 oz) belly pork
2 egg yolks
100 g (4 oz) almonds or hazelnuts, lightly toasted
100 g (4 oz) fine-cut streaky bacon (without rind) or pork fat
2 bay leaves

The evening before, strip all the meat from the birds and the rabbit – they should yield about 700 g (1½ lb) of meat. Leave the breast and back fillets whole, dice the rest and put all into a bowl. Work the lemon rind, juniper berries, herbs, salt and pepper into the meat and pour in the wine and whisky. Mix well and leave to marinate overnight in a cool place.

Next day, take out the whole fillets and reserve them. Mince the rest of the meat with the belly pork. Work in the egg yolks and the nuts. If you prefer not to stick an enquiring finger into the raw mix to taste it, you could fry a little bit of it to check the seasoning.

Line a terrine dish or 20 x 10 cm (8 x 4 inch) loaf tin with bacon or thin strips of pork fat, leaving enough to fold over the top. Spread in half the minced meat and arrange the whole fillets over it. Finish with the rest of the minced meat. Place a couple of bay leaves on top and fold over the bacon. Cover with foil.

Cook in a *bain-marie* (a roasting tin half filled with boiling water) in the oven at 180°C (350°F) mark 4 for 1¼–1½ hours. It may take longer depending on the age and toughness of the raw materials. Check by pricking with a knife; if the juices run clear, the meat is tender. Leave to cool. Potted Grabbit keeps well for 2 weeks in the refrigerator. Serve as a first course, with either redcurrant or rowan jelly as an accompaniment.

Venison with Redcurrant Gravy

Venison is a dry, lean meat and needs plenty of marination. In the marinade, Cherry uses green juniper berries from her own tree. A 1.4–1.8 kg (3–4 lb) boned and rolled joint might suit a small family better: allow 15 minutes per 450 g (1 lb) plus 15 minutes extra.

Serves 3 family meals

5.6–6.4 kg (12–14 lb) haunch or
   shoulder of venison on the bone
150 ml (¼ pint) olive oil
10–15 ml (2–3 tsp) salt
15–30 ml (1–2 tbsp) juniper berries
sprigs of tarragon, lemon thyme
   and parsley

30 ml (2 tbsp) redcurrant jelly
2 glasses red wine

To serve
sauté potatoes

Wipe the joint and rub it with the oil and salt. Settle it in a large roasting tin. Sprinkle with the juniper berries and herbs, wrap in foil and leave to marinate overnight.

Next day, roast the joint, still covered with foil, in the oven at 180°C (350°F) mark 4, allowing 15 minutes per 450 g (1 lb). With a joint weighing over 10 lb, you should *deduct* 15 minutes from the overall cooking time rather than adding on. Thirty minutes before the end of cooking, remove the foil and turn the oven up to brown the joint. After 15 minutes, test with a skewer pushed right to the bone – if you like your venison rare, the juices should run pink. Pour off and reserve the juices – there will be plenty.

Meanwhile, skim off the oil from the juices, and use it to sauté some parboiled potatoes (the oven will be quite full enough). Boil down the remaining juices until you are left with about 450 ml (¾ pint). Stir in the redcurrant jelly and wine and bubble everything up in the roasting tin, scraping off all the delicious sticky brown bits to make a dark rich gravy.

Let the joint rest for 20 minutes after you have taken it out of the oven – it will be much easier to carve. Serve surrounded by vegetables and sauté potatoes, with the gravy and more redcurrant jelly handed separately.

Peach and Apricot Tart

Catherine, the youngest Drummond daughter, makes the autumn crop of quinces into a lovely rose-amber jelly used to glaze the peaches and apricots in the family's favourite tart.

Serves 6

The base
225 g (8 oz) digestive biscuits
**100 g (4 oz) butter or margarine,
    softened**
25 g (1 oz) sugar
25 g (1 oz) ground almonds

Fudge filling
100 g (4 oz) can condensed milk
100 g (4 oz) golden syrup

100 g (4 oz) butter or margarine
50 g (2 oz) sugar

The topping
3–4 ripe peaches
3–4 ripe apricots
**45–60 ml (3–4 tbsp) quince jelly
    (any clear jelly will do)**

Crush the biscuits and mash in the butter and sugar. Press the mixture into a large tart tin. Sprinkle the almonds over the top.

Melt all the filling ingredients in a saucepan and bubble it up for 5 minutes until it is a soft toffee consistency. Pour the filling over the digestive crumble.

Scald, peel and slice the peaches. Stone the apricots (peel them if you like) and slice them. Arrange the peach slices in a cartwheel on the filling, starting on the outer rim. Finish off with a centre of apricot slices. Warm the quince jelly until just liquid, and trickle it over to glaze the fruit.

Ginger-Spiced Pumpkin Purée

Serves 6

900 g (2 lb) pumpkin (prepared
  weight)
50–75 g (2–3 oz) butter

10 ml (2 tsp) ground ginger
salt and plenty of black pepper

Peel the pumpkin and remove the cottony middle and seeds. Cook in a lidded saucepan half filled with water – it will take 20–25 minutes to soften completely. Drain and mash.

Return the mashed pumpkin to a gentle heat, stir in the butter and ginger and seasonings. Leave on the heat to dry out all the moisture. Pile into a pretty dish and serve hot.

Tomato Chutney

Serves 2.8 kg (6 lb)

1.8 kg (4 lb) tomatoes, scalded and
  skinned
4 medium onions, skinned and
  finely chopped
600 ml (1 pint) malt wine vinegar
225 g (8 oz) sugar (more if the
  tomatoes are green)
10 ml (2 tsp) salt

5 ml (1 tsp) crushed peppercorns
10 ml (2 tsp) coriander seeds (fresh
  from the garden if you grow your
  own)
8 cloves (more if you like the
  flavour)
10 ml (2 tsp) mustard seeds

Put all the ingredients into a large saucepan and bring the mixture to the boil. Simmer gently, stirring regularly, for about 2 hours until the mixture is thick and jammy. Fill warm sterilised jam jars. Cover and seal when cool. It is ready immediately, but improves with keeping.

Breakfast Pancakes with Herbs

Scotch pancakes are quickly made. Cherry mixes her batter with fresh herbs and fries the pancakes in pan drippings for a delicious morning flavour.

Serves 12

225 g (8 oz) plain flour
salt and pepper
7.5 ml (1½ tsp) cream of tartar
5 ml (1 tsp) bicarbonate of soda
1 egg
300 ml (½ pint) milk (soured is
    best)

60 ml (4 tbsp) finely chopped mixed
    herbs – lemon thyme, chives,
    parsley, marjoram, tarragon
a little bacon fat or the frying from
    good sausages

Mix the flour with a pinch of salt, the cream of tartar and bicarbonate of soda. Make a dip in the flour, break in the egg and pour in the milk. Work it all into a smooth batter – it should be thicker than a pancake batter and wetter than a cake mix. Stir in the chopped herbs until well mixed and season with salt and pepper. You can do the whole operation in the blender if you prefer.

Melt a knob of the fat on a griddle or in a large heavy frying pan. Once it is hot and lightly hazed with blue, drop on ladlefuls of the batter.

When the surfaces of the pancakes are dry and full of holes, turn them over and cook the other side. Serve the pancakes hot from the pan – they're lovely with sausages and bacon.

THE UNEXPECTED GUEST

I can never resist the lure of the unexpected guest. However carefully I organise my entertaining, there are always a couple more than my table can comfortably accommodate. I used to think the problem was logistical. Matters might be solved, I reasoned, by a larger table, smaller chairs, thinner guests with neater elbows. Twenty years and as many permutations of furniture and figure have not solved anything. The telephone rings. The doorbell goes. And there we are again – a tidy dinner party for eight guests, more or less neatly matched with the prescribed ratio of males to females, turns into an untidy bunfight for 13.

The household's catering problem is compounded by a shifting population of permanently ravenous young adults, for some of whom I acknowledge responsibility – others are more transient. Add to that an extraordinary family talent, when country-based, for choosing the one house right at the end of the mud track with nothing but an irritable bull for a neighbour, and weekend catering can be a high-risk business.

An imbalance of diners to dinner remains the only constant in my household. I think it must be because I like it that way. There's challenge in the task of converting a chicken into a meal for a baker's dozen. The daintily dressed dining table is not within my grasp. Guests are accommodated on chairs fetched from all over the house. An extra 18 inches is added to the available elbow room by a hall table of, miraculously, the same height and width as my dining room table.

The soon-to-be-groaning board is covered with an old blanket and a clean, white cotton sheet (easy to bleach out stains) – I like the feel of thick, soft cloth on a dining table far better than polished wood. This, along with my collection of pretty but unmatched side plates, a sufficient quantity of generously-sized wine glasses, sets the dinner scene for comfort rather than elegance. I rarely have flowers and candles as I like to put the food on the table in serving dishes.

I use my larder to augment any shortcomings I have in my fresh-food shopping. In it I keep a few regular stores. Two or three pasta shapes, beans and rice provide the bulk. Beans do need forethought as they have to be soaked, so I usually have a tin or two of ready-cooked. Three oils: soya or sunflower for frying, olive oil for mayonnaise and for saucing pasta and Mediterranean dishes, and a nut oil (hazelnut is my favourite) for green salads. Plus good vinegar – my current favourite is 25-year-old sherry vinegar which has a powerful mellow flavour.

The first course at my table is nearly always something to be eaten with the fingers – plenty of napkins provided, but nevertheless an essentially messy performance. It might be raw vegetables with a garlic mayonnaise for dipping, or little pizzas, home-made with slices of French bread, or crab warmed in olive oil with garlic and chilli.

For the second course, vegetables, sauces and salads go straight on to the table. The main dish I usually serve out myself from a side table, particularly if I've chosen a large poached fish (farmed salmon for price, sea-trout for flavour) or a shoulder of lamb – my favourite joint, particularly when cooked with a great deal of garlic, *en pistache*. I like to make a pudding for a party: it might be an almond cake soaked in alcohol-flavoured syrup like a baba, or profiteroles.

When cooking for a multitude, it's best to keep it simple: loaves and fishes have always had greater crowd-appeal than vegetable terrine and pigeon breasts with raspberry vinegar.

Apple Harvest

The Golden Valley is Herefordshire's horn of plenty. Bounded by the old market towns of Hereford, Abergavenny and Hay-on-Wye, it is at its best in autumn when orchards are full of fruit and the harvest is on its way home.

At the southern end of the triangle, in the shadow of the Black Hill, Charis Ward and her daughter Sarah Sage have taken 23 years to restore the gardens and home-farm of Abbey Dore Court to productive glory.

These days a stroll round the beautiful gardens and plant nursery can be followed by lunch or tea in the converted stables.

Locals still bake the old-fashioned raised pies traditionally associated with market day. Usual fillings include richly spiced pork, juicy mutton, veal-and-ham slotted through with a line of orange-yolked eggs; a fine meal for a crisp autumn midday, to be taken sitting on an old stone wall, and best washed down with knife-sharp new cider drawn from the keg.

This is apple country. Relative newcomers to the area, Susie and Ivor Dunkerton of Hayn Hood, Luntley, near Pembridge, make sophisticated one-variety ciders and perry, too. They have plenty of appreciative customers who supply them with rare old cider apples.

'We started the single-apple ciders because we didn't know the flavours of the different apples,' Susie explains. 'So we had to taste them all individually in order to get the right blend – and some of them were fine on their own.'

Mint and Apple Chutney

Charis Ward's apple trees were chosen to give a good long cropping season: Howgate Wonder, Laxton's Fortune, Tidyman's Early Worcester, George Cave, with the Coxes at the tail end. For baking, Charis grows The Reverend E. Wilkes: 'He's lovely baked with flaked tapioca and syrup in the core.' The best keeping-apples are Crispin and Winston. Any imperfect fruit is made into chutney: this fresh-flavoured green version is excellent with mutton pies, washed down with a draught of Dunkerton's single-apple cider – Kingston Black or the sharp, bright Breakwells Seedling.

Makes about 2.8 kg (6 lb)

450 g (1 lb) apples, peeled, cored and chopped
mint leaves to fill a 600 ml (1 pint) jug, chopped
450 g (1 lb) onions, skinned and chopped
450 g (1 lb) seedless raisins

225 g (8 oz) tomatoes, scalded and skinned (green ones are best)
450 g (1 lb) sugar
600 ml (1 pint) cider vinegar
30 ml (2 tbsp) mustard seeds
10 ml (2 tsp) salt
5 ml (1 tsp) ground white pepper

Put all the ingredients in a heavy saucepan and bring to the boil. Cover and simmer for 2 hours, until thick, then pot in sterilised jars.

Abbey Dore Marrow and Tomato Soup

A few of Sarah's tender young courgettes inevitably grow into prize monsters. She makes them into this cheerful autumn soup, using up the final well-ripened crop of odd-sized tomatoes from the greenhouse.

Serves 4–6

900 g (2 lb) marrow, peeled, deseeded and roughly chopped
900 g (2 lb) tomatoes, scalded, skinned and roughly chopped
450 g (1 lb) onions, skinned and chopped
1–2 outside celery stalks, sliced

600 ml (1 pint) stock or water
handful of fresh basil leaves
salt and pepper

To finish
30 ml (2 tbsp) double cream

Put all the ingredients except the cream into a large saucepan. Bring to the boil, cover and simmer for 30 minutes until the vegetables are all soft and soupy. Mash everything down with a potato masher. Finish with a swirl of cream.

Little Spiced Lamb and Apple Pies

This is a delicious variation on a mutton pie. Each is a lovely fistful and delicious served with Mint and Apple Chutney (page 102).

Serves 8

700 g (1½ lb) boneless stewing lamb	2.5 ml (½ tsp) ground cloves
1 large cooking apple, peeled, cored and chopped	5 ml (1 tsp) salt
	5 ml (1 tsp) pepper
25 g (1 oz) sultanas or raisins	hot-water crust pastry (see Spiced Pork Pie with Eggs, page 104)
5 ml (1 tsp) grated lemon rind	flour for dusting

Chop the lamb, fat and all, finely (don't mince it); mix with the apple, sultanas, lemon rind, cloves, salt and pepper.

Divide the pastry into eight dough balls and work on one at a time; keep the rest in a bowl set over hot water and covered with a damp cloth. Reserve a quarter of the first dough ball and roll out the rest into a neat circle about 20 cm (8 inches) in diameter.

Dust the pastry with flour and place it, floured side down, on an upturned clean jam jar. Press the edges round the jar to give a neat little pie base. As soon as it is cold and firm (a minute or two), reverse the jar and ease off the pie base. Pack in enough stuffing to come nearly to the top, pressing it well down.

Roll out the remaining quarter of pastry to make a lid, allowing an extra 1 cm (½ inch) margin. Damp the edges of the pastry and lay on the lid, raising the edges and pressing them together to form a rim. Lightly prick the lid. Make all the pies. Transfer them to a baking sheet.

Bake in the oven at 200°C (400°F) mark 6 for 30 minutes; reduce the heat to 190°C (375°F) mark 5 for 15–25 minutes until the pastry is set.

Spiced Pork Pie with Eggs

A hot-water crust is the traditional pastry for a raised pie. The pie needs a sturdy dough that seals in all the meat juices and stands up to the long cooking. Hot-water crust was used for the enormous game pies that landowners had sent to London from their country estates in pre-refrigeration days. Everything had to stand up to horse-and-carriage transport.

Serves 8

For the pastry
450 g (1 lb) plain flour
5 ml (1 tsp) salt
225 ml (8 fl oz) water
175 g (6 oz) lard
egg and milk, to glaze

For the filling
1–2 trotters and 900 g (2 lb) bones for the jellied stock
fresh herbs
225 g (8 oz) belly pork without rind (use the rind to help jelly the stock)

450 g (1 lb) lean pork
225 g (8 oz) uncooked gammon or lean bacon
5 ml (1 tsp) dried thyme
1–2 sage leaves, crumbled or chopped
5 ml (1 tsp) ground allspice
5 ml (1 tsp) ground nutmeg
2.5 ml (1/2 tsp) pepper
5 ml (1 tsp) salt
3 hard-boiled eggs, shelled

Put the trotters and bones in a saucepan with a few potherbs, the pork rind and water to cover. Bring to the boil and leave to simmer for 3–4 hours to reduce to 600 ml (1 pint) of strong stock. Strain through a jelly cloth. The stock will set firm.

Make the pastry. Sift the flour with the salt. Bring the water to the boil in a large saucepan with the lard, and boil until the fat melts. Beat in the flour and cook over a low heat until the paste comes away from the sides of the pan. This is a hot-water pastry and at this point it will look slightly trans-parent. Tip it out on to a well-floured board and, as soon as it is cool enough to handle, knead it thoroughly until it is alabaster-smooth. Put the pastry to prove in a warm place for 30 minutes; keep it warm in a plastic bag. Work quickly once the pastry is out in the air – it will crack if it is allowed to cool. The temperature is important; if it is too cold the pastry will break and crumble when raised; if it is too soft (either too warm or too much fat in the mix), it will fall away from the sides of the pie mould.

Chop the pork and gammon or bacon together (don't mince them), and season well with the herbs, spices, salt and pepper. Grease a 25 x 10 cm (10 x 4 inch) loaf tin, preferably one with a removable base. The tin should be at least 7.5 cm (3 inches) deep. If you have one of those lovely, hinged, oval pie-moulds, so much the better.

Cut off a quarter of the pastry and reserve it for the lid, keeping it warm. If using a loaf tin; roll out the larger piece quickly with a rolling pin and press it firmly into the base and up the sides of the well-greased tin. If using a hinged oval mould, roll out the large piece of dough into a circle which is thin at the edges and much fatter in the middle. Fold the dough in half into a semi-circle and roll out the fat part to make a pouch or pocket. It will now look like a folded sunhat. Slip your hand inside the double thickness and ease out the pocket – the 'crown' of the hat. Drop it gently into the greased pie mould, with the crown lining the base and the rim gently eased up the sides.

Pack in one-third of the meat, pressing well down. Lay in the shelled eggs, end to end. Pack round with the remaining meat. Roll out the small er piece of pastry to cover the pie, damping the edges of the pastry and pressing them together with a fork. Trim, decorate with pastry leaves and glaze with a mixture of egg and milk.

Bake in the oven at 200°C (400°F) mark 6 for 45 minutes. Reduce to 180°C (350°F) mark 4 and bake for 1½–2 hours longer until the crust is nicely brown and the filling juices run clear. If you use a meat thermometer, the reading should be 75°C/170°F.

Let the pie settle for 10 minutes before you unmould it. When the pie is quite cold, funnel in enough hot jellied stock to fill up all the gaps – the filling always shrinks during the cooking. The pie should accept 300–450 ml (½–¾ pint). It is ready to eat when the stock has set.

Decorate the pie with a sprig of sage to indicate it has a pork filling (a veal pie might have a sprig of parsley).

Duck with Apples and Calvados

This recipe comes from Sarah's godmother, who uses a pheasant that has been roughly shot and will not do for hanging and roasting. Wild duck, mallard in particular, is delicious cooked like this. Water birds should not be hung, but plucked and cooked within 24 hours of being shot. The saffron adds a lovely fragrance.

Serves 4–6

1 domestic duck (or 2 wild ones)
handful of fresh herbs
700 g (1½ lb) apples
30 ml (2 tbsp) flour
25 g (1 oz) butter
2 medium onions, skinned
    and chopped
300 ml (½ pint) apple wine or dry
    cider
2 celery stalks, chopped

1–2 bay leaves
parsley
5–6 saffron threads
salt and pepper

To finish
30 ml (2 tbsp) Calvados or brandy
butter for frying
45–60 ml (3–4 tbsp) double cream

Joint the bird(s). Put the back and giblets with a few herbs in a pan with enough water to cover. Boil until you have 600 ml (1 pint) stock.

Peel, core and slice all but 1 apple. Coat the joints in flour and heat the butter in a flameproof casserole. Fry the onions and the duck pieces over a high heat until they colour. Add 300 ml (½ pint) stock and the apple wine or cider. Stir in the celery and herbs and bubble up. Add the saffron, soaked for 10 minutes in a little hot water and crushed, and the sliced, peeled apples. Pour in enough stock to cover all the duck pieces, season and bring back to the boil. Cover and simmer for 45–60 minutes until the meat is tender.

Remove the duck pieces, vegetables and apples, and arrange them on a warm dish. Boil the sauce down for a few minutes over a fierce heat until it is thick and rich. Warm the Calvados; pour it over the duck and set light to it.

Slice the remaining apple finely and fry quickly in a little butter. Add the cream to the sauce; bubble up and pour over the duck. Garnish with the fried apple slices.

Cornfields
and orchards,

Bakeday at Little Cornard

hedgerows lively with game and sweet herbs, fine fat geese, pigs and thick-fleeced sheep for the wool trade – there's little that will not flourish in the rich earth of Suffolk. East Anglia has always been prosperous – too prosperous, sometimes, for the peace of its inhabitants. The Angles and Saxons, Vikings and Danes all raided the store-cupboard in turn.

Like most farming communities in Suffolk, Little Cornard is an ancient settlement. I was assured there were still some people who've never left Little Cornard, never even been to Sudbury. The village is not on the way to anywhere – unless, perhaps, to Great Cornard, the village made famous by Gainsborough's painting. The land breeds artists as well as farmers: John Constable was born near here, among just such tree-shadowed hayfields, under those same wide skies banked with billowing clouds.

Barbara and Eddie Johnson were both born and bred within 20 miles of Little Cornard. Now they farm 360 acres of mixed arable from a spick-and-span farmhouse on the outskirts of the village.

'Pigeon pie used to be a real treat, or maybe starling or rook. My husband Eddie loves pigeon. On our silver wedding our three married sons came for a meal. I cooked about 50 pigeons, and they said: "Oh, lovely quail." I laughed and told them it was Cornard quail.'

Zillah Wallace has similar memories of her childhood. She lives in a pretty cottage along Spout Lane, a steep hedgerow-lined creek down which an errant spring bounces and gurgles every winter. Her pride and joy is her trim cottage garden with its Lady Heneker apple tree. 'We had lovely old-fashioned apples when I was a child, and grew all our vegetables.

'Monday was washday, Tuesday ironing, Friday bakeday. Mother had certain places in the ovens for whatever she was cooking. If it was too hot you could get the heat down by painting the walls with a sack on a pole dipped in a bucket of cold water. Usually on bakeday we had dumplings made with yeast dough – we ate them with a sweet white sauce. Smoked fish was the tea-time treat. Grandpa Ben used to like his bloaters toasted in a grill over the fire. The fat sizzles as they cook, and makes a lovely crisp fishy smell.'

Along the old parish track at Sawyers Farm – with Ronald Blythe, author of *Akenfield*, as a neighbour – live Caroline and John Stevens. Their Elizabethan brick-and-timber farmhouse is lapped by a sea of herbs and wild flowers – the raw materials for Suffolk Herbs, the Stevens' pioneering seed and plant business. After 16 years, Caroline now feels very much part of the local community. The best moments are to be had when the work is done, over a meal, round the big table in Caroline's comfortable oak-beamed kitchen. There's a tradition of yarn-spinning among the villagers of Suffolk. So the group – fuelled by Mrs Davey's rabbit pie and Barbara Johnson's stewed pigeons – settles itself down with a glass of Mrs Good-child's wine, to swap stories of the old times, both good and bad.

Cornard 'Quail' with Vegetables

Barbara Johnson's recipe relies on long, slow cooking to tenderise the pigeons – old or young, they have a lovely flavour. If you don't care to pluck the birds, skin them (feathers and all) or just use the breasts. The stew is cooked on top of the stove – even as late as the 1930s many people did not have ovens, and so the Sunday dinner would be carried to the baker for cooking.

Serves 4

6 pigeons, cleaned and plucked
plenty of black pepper
15 ml (1 tbsp) good beef dripping
2–3 medium onions, skinned and
   sliced
3–4 mature carrots, peeled and
   chopped

2–3 smallish turnips, peeled
5 ml (1 tsp) dried thyme
2.5 ml (1/2 tsp) dried sage
salt
30 ml (2 tbsp) chopped fresh
   parsley

Split the pigeons in half, or leave them whole, as you please. Pepper them thoroughly. Melt the dripping in a heavy casserole, add the birds and turn in the hot fat for a few moments. Push them aside and fry the onions until they soften and take a little colour.

Pack in the rest of the vegetables, add the thyme, sage and salt, and pour in enough water to cover the birds. Bring to the boil, turn down the heat, put the lid on tightly and simmer gently for at least 3 hours until the pigeons are quite tender. Check every now and then and top up with boiling water if necessary.

Take off the lid at the end, and boil for a few minutes to reduce the gravy. Garnish with a sprinkle of parsley. Serve with creamed and baked potatoes or Brussels sprouts.

Rabbit Pie

Mrs Davey's rabbit pie is one of the treats of harvest time, when plenty of rabbits are caught as they run in front of the combines. In the old days, reaping was done in formation, with a special rhythm and songs to keep the line advancing. The rabbits should be 'hulked' – paunched – as soon as they are shot. Skinning can wait: for two days in summer, three days in the autumn, a week in winter. Young rabbit skins easily – older ones are harder.

Serves 6

2 rabbits, skinned and wiped
225 g (8 oz) fat-and-lean fresh belly
   pork (take the rind off and give it
   to the birds)
2 medium onions, skinned and
   chopped
1 bay leaf, 3–4 sage leaves and
   1 sprig thyme, tied in a muslin
   bag
300 ml (½ pint) water

For the pastry
275 g (10 oz) plain flour
2.5 ml (½ tsp) salt
150 g (5 oz) lard
15–30 ml (1–2 tbsp) ice-cold water
milk, to glaze

Start well ahead, as the filling has to cool before you can put on the pastry. Joint the rabbit into eight pieces. Dice the pork belly. Put rabbit, pork belly, onions, herbs and water into a flameproof casserole or a saucepan. Bring to the boil, turn down the heat, put the lid on tightly and leave to cook gently either on top of the stove, or in the oven at 170°C (325°F) mark 3 for 1¼–1½ hours until the rabbit is quite tender. Check every now and then and add a little extra hot water if the stew looks like drying out. Tip the rabbit into a pie dish (remove the herb bag) and leave the stew to cool.

Make the pastry. Sift the flour with the salt, and rub in the fat as lightly as you can, lifting to let the air in. Work in enough water to make a soft dough – the less water used, the lighter the pastry.

Roll the pastry out on a very lightly floured board, into a round of the correct size and shape to fit over the pie dish comfortably without stretching. Dampen the edges of the dish and lay on the pastry lid. Decorate with pastry leaves and brush the top of the pie with milk to glaze.

Bake in the oven at 200°C (400°F) mark 6 for 45 minutes until the crust is crisp and golden. Serve with swedes and potatoes mashed together with butter and milk.

Wholegrain Mustard with Honey

Look for the mustard seeds in your local wholefood store. The best mix is black and white seeds in the proportion roughly 3:5 of black to white.

Makes about 450 ml (³/₄ pint)

225 g (8 oz) mustard seeds   **30 ml (2 tbsp) honey**
300 ml (¹/₂ pint) vinegar   **15 ml (1 tbsp) ground cinnamon**

Steep the mustard seeds in half the vinegar overnight. Next day, pound everything up in a mortar with the honey and cinnamon.

Mix it to a stiff paste with the rest of the vinegar – you may need more or less.

Pot and cover, but do not seal it for a day or two, until you are sure the mustard will not expand further and need more vinegar.

Salt-Fried Bloaters

Fish is the high spot of a Suffolk tea. The main meal is traditionally taken in the middle of the day, around 1 o'clock so high tea is the second most important meal. Yarmouth bloaters and sprats are the local tea-time speciality – there used to be plenty of smoke-houses at Yarmouth, with salt from the Essex marshes providing the other essential. Until the 1940s and 1950s there were vast shoals of herring and an immense herring fleet. Herrings were brought to the villages in little trains, in trucks loaded with ice. Every village could be reached from the railway station – locals remember that you could smell the fish wagon for miles.

Allow 1 bloater per person. Sprinkle a heavy iron frying-pan with salt. Heat the pan until it is lightly smoking. Then fry the bloaters in their own fat – it'll be drawn out by the salt. Give them about 3–4 minutes each side.

They are delicious served with a little cold butter to melt into the hot flesh. The same method can be followed with sprats – they are nice finished with finely chopped parsley.

Suffolk Yeast Rusks

Makes 24 split rusks

700 g (1½ lb) plain flour	15 g (½ oz) fresh yeast or 10 ml
5 ml (1 tsp) salt	(2 tsp) dried yeast
300 ml (½ pint) tepid milk or milk	2.5 ml (½ tsp) sugar
and water	100 g (4 oz) butter

Sift the flour with the salt. Put the warm milk or milk and water into a jug and mix in the yeast and sugar. Leave for 5 minutes until it froths up. Rub the butter into the flour. Work in the yeast liquid gradually until you have a soft dough. Work until smooth.

Put the dough to rise in a warm place, in a bowl covered with a clean damp cloth or cling-film, until it has doubled in size. Knead well to distribute air bubbles. Knuckle the dough out to a thickness of 1 cm (1/2 inch) and cut into rounds, using a 5–6 cm (2–2 1/2 inch) cutter.

Bake in the oven at 230°C (450°F) mark 8 for about 10–12 minutes until brown. Take the rusks out and split them in two. Return them to a cooler oven, 180°C (350°F) mark 4, and continue baking for a further 12–15 minutes until they are hard and crisp.

SUFFOLK YEAST RUSKS

For an extra taste of Suffolk, poach a few rounds of the dough in simmering water and serve with a lemon or vanilla cream sauce or custard. These dumplings are known as 'swimmers'.

Old English Salad Cream

This salad cream is Zillah's family recipe – made with eggs from their own hens.

Makes 2 servings

yolks of 2 hard-boiled eggs	**1.25 ml (1/4 tsp) pepper**
5 ml (1 tsp) sugar	**30 ml (2 tbsp) cream**
2.5 ml (1/2 tsp) made mustard	**15 ml (1 tbsp) vinegar**
2.5 ml (1/2 tsp) salt	

Bruise the egg yolks with a wooden spoon and add the sugar, mustard, salt and pepper. Work in the cream gradually. When the mixture is perfectly smooth, add the vinegar drop by drop, stirring briskly.

Serve with a mixed salad, and use the whites of the eggs as a garnish.

Bread Pudding

Ronald Blythe remembers that bread pudding could be bought from little bakers' carts. It was sold in big slabs – fine for hungry lads after a day's harvesting.

Serves 5–6

450 g (1 lb) old bread (brown or white)

about 900 ml (1½ pints) boiling water or milk

5 ml (1 tsp) each grated nutmeg, ground cinnamon, ginger and cloves

100 g (4 oz) mixed dried fruit (include a few dates – and maybe chopped walnuts too)

100 g (4 oz) brown sugar (optional)

extra ground cinnamon for dusting

Crumble the bread into a large bowl. Soak the crumbs with boiling water or milk, leave to cool, then squeeze out excess water with your hands. Work the bread to remove any lumps and mix in the spices, dried fruit and sugar, if using.

Butter a large roasting dish, spread the mixture in the dish in a smooth layer and finish with an extra dusting of cinnamon. Bake in the oven at 180°C (350°F) mark 4 for 45–50 minutes.

Gypsy Pudding

Barbara Johnson prefers this version. It's also known as Manchester Pudding and Queen of Puddings, and many more names besides.

Serves 4

300 ml (½ pint) milk

300 ml (½ pint) single cream

15 ml (1 tbsp) brandy

2 eggs

50 g (2 oz) sugar

5 ml (1 tsp) grated lemon rind

100 g (4 oz) finely grated fresh breadcrumbs

45–60 ml (3–4 tbsp) damson or blackcurrant jam (the sharper the better)

To serve

thick cream

B eat the milk and cream with the brandy, eggs, sugar and lemon rind. Stir in the breadcrumbs. Spread the jam in the bottom of a pie dish. Pour the breadcrumb and custard mixture over the top, then bake in the oven at 180°C (350°F) mark 4 for 25–30 minutes until set and golden. Serve with thick cream.

Bread and Butter Pudding

Zillah likes this more luxurious version. It makes a fine finish to a leisurely autumn Sunday lunch. Use single cream instead of milk to make an even richer dish.

Serves 4

4–5 slices buttered bread	50 g (2 oz) sugar
75 g (3 oz) currants soaked in orange juice or brandy	grated nutmeg
15 ml (1 tbsp) chopped crystallised ginger	To serve
	thick cream
600 ml (1 pint) milk	brown sugar
3 eggs	

P ut a layer of bread in the bottom of a small pie dish. Sprinkle with currants and ginger. Finish with layers of the rest of the bread and dried fruit. The last bread layer must be arranged buttered-side-up.

Beat the milk with the eggs and 25 g (1 oz) of the sugar and pour this custard over the bread. Sprinkle with the rest of the sugar and finish with a dusting of nutmeg. Bake in the oven at 180°C (350°F) mark 4 for 25–30 minutes until well-glazed and set. Serve with thick cream and brown sugar.

Autumn in Wales

The post-office-cum-shop in Rosebush in Dyfed, South Wales is flanked by a neat terrace of gaily painted two-up-two-downs which once sheltered the quarry workers from the now worked-out Welsh slate quarries in the hills behind, and their families. Beyond stretches the road to the quarry workings. Crags and cliffs of broken slate and rock, patch-worked with heather and turf and berry-laden scrub, make an intimate, small-hill landscape to cradle the village.

Run by Dorothy and David Thomas, it is a clearing-house and meeting place for the village. An old lady comes in for a special order of Dorothy's sponge-cakes, and stays to discuss the impending arrival of a grandson. In the shop Dorothy sells her own bread and Welsh cheeses, as well as the usual groceries and locally grown vegetables – leeks, courgettes, beans, cabbages, calabrese and potatoes.

Behind the shop is the popular tea-room Dorothy opened (once a week it doubles as the doctor's surgery). Welsh cakes, scones and home-made jams delight the hillwalkers and tourists. The white walls are furnished with old farm implements and memorabilia from the railway once intended to link Rosebush with Fishguard. Displayed against the old brick oven is a collection of delicately curved loving-spoons carved out of elm – the traditional betrothal gifts from young men to their sweethearts. On the other side of the house, Dorothy has opened a bar serving small meals of starters and sweets, and a dining room. The menu is varied and international: chicken with lemon and coriander; salmon with a seafood and laverbread sauce.

Rosebush is some 10 miles from the nearest coast – Fishguard is the closest source of fresh fish. And Dorothy makes the occasional trip down the soft green valleys through Carmarthen to buy cockles and laverbread from Penclawdd. She freezes the laverbread in two- to four-ounce portions and uses it to flavour her seafood dishes. Her supplier, Chris Howells, is the latest of a long line of Penclawdd cockle-women, whose laverbread and cockle 'factory' is housed in a hut beside the windswept Loughor estuary.

Cockles are prepared in tandem with laverbread, using the same equipment. The silky, hair-like seaweed has to be cooked until very soft – about four hours. Chris judges the moment the laverbread is ready by experience – it may vary according to the time of year. The thick green-brown purée is then ladled into cartons or small plastic bags and sold by the cockle-merchants. Locally this rich soup is likely to be heated up and served on fried bread as part of a breakfast or teatime fry-up.

Times have changed at Penclawdd. Steel vats have replaced the old iron cauldrons. Tractors and trailers do the work of the traditional pony-and-cart. Now the old men sit out of an evening on benches where dozens of cockle and laverbread factories once mushroomed at the edge of the mud-flats. Nonetheless, the cookery of Wales makes use of its own special ingredients and remains firmly rooted in its own traditions.

Laverbread and Crab Soufflés with Cockle Sauce

The delicate flavour of fresh crab is underlined in this recipe by the sea-and-mineral flavour of the seaweed. Puréed spinach and a few tablespoons of cockle or clam juice can substitute.

Serves 8

For the soufflés
1 boiled crab or 175 g (6 oz)
   prepared crabmeat
50 g (2 oz) butter
50 g (2 oz) plain flour
450 ml (³/4 pint) milk
175 g (6 oz) prepared laverbread
salt and pepper
2.5 ml (¹/2 tsp) grated nutmeg
3 eggs, separated

For the cockle sauce
150 ml (¹/4 pint) white sauce from
   soufflé mix
150 ml (¹/4 pint) whipping cream
100 g (4 oz) cockles or clams,
   shelled
50 g (2 oz) prepared laverbread

If the crab is whole, pull the body apart and pick out all the meat – discarding only the mouthpiece and the grey feathery 'dead man's fingers' that fringe the inside carapace.

Make the white sauce: melt the butter in a small saucepan. Stir in the flour and cook gently until the mixture is still pale but sandy. Whisk in the milk slowly, beating till you have a thick sauce. Simmer for about 5 minutes, then set aside 150 ml (¹/4 pint) of the sauce.

Stir the crabmeat and prepared laverbread into the remaining sauce. Season with salt, pepper and nutmeg.

Beat the egg whites until quite stiff. By now the sauce will be cool enough to stir in the yolks. Fold in the whites. Taste and adjust the seasoning. Butter eight small soufflé dishes and spoon in the mixture, leaving a finger's width for expansion. Bake in the oven at 200°C (400°F) mark 6 for 10–12 minutes until puffed up and golden.

Meanwhile make the cockle sauce. Heat up the reserved white sauce with the cream. Stir in the cockles and laverbread. Season with the salt and pepper. Serve with the soufflés as soon as they are ready.

LAVERBREAD

Laverbread is available in cans from some grocers, but it can also be bought in pressed, dried form from health-food stores and oriental supermarkets under the Japanese name of nori. Soak 15 g (1/2 oz) in 300 ml (1/2 pint) warm water for 30 minutes.

Cocklecakes with Laverbread

Cocklecakes are really batter fritters – and a favourite way for the cocklewomen of Penclawdd to prepare the harvest of the mud-flats. Traditionally they were shallow-fried in bacon fat.

Serves 4 as a light supper

225 g (8 oz) plain flour
1 egg, separated
15 ml (1 tbsp) vegetable oil
300 ml (1/2 pint) warm water
225 g (8 oz) cockles or clams,
  shelled

salt
30–45 ml (3–4 tbsp) chopped fresh
  parsley
oil for frying
225 g (8 oz) prepared laverbread
juice of 1/2 lemon

Sift the flour into a bowl. Work the egg yolk and oil into the flour and beat in the water gradually until you have a thick batter. Whisk and leave aside for 30 minutes.

Whisk the egg white until stiff and stir into the batter. Add the cockles, then the salt and parsley. Heat two fingers of oil in a heavy pan. Deep fry spoonfuls of the batter until the cakes are golden and crisp. Heat up the laverbread with the lemon juice. Serve both together piping hot, with wedges of lemon.

Bacon Cawl with Three Sauces

The *cawl* can be served as a whole feast, starting with the broth and its vegetables, with the meat and potatoes served as the second course. The traditional accompaniment to the bacon is a parsley sauce. One or all of the three sauces given below makes a truly delicious alternative.

Serves 4

For the cawl
700 g (1½ lb) collar bacon with rind (or shin of beef or salt beef)
1.8 litres (3 pints) water

For the vegetables
700 g (1½ lb) potatoes
1 small swede
3–4 mature carrots, or other seasonal vegetables
2 large leeks or spring onions
30 ml (2 tbsp) chopped fresh parsley

For the mustard and egg sauce
50 g (2 oz) butter
25 g (1 oz) plain flour
5 ml (1 tsp) mustard powder
2.5 ml (½ tsp) turmeric
300 ml (½ pint) cawl stock and milk mixed
1 hard-boiled egg
15 ml (1 tbsp) vinegar
salt and pepper

For the spiced tomato ketchup
450 g (1 lb) ripe tomatoes, skinned
1 small onion, skinned and chopped
5 ml (1 tsp) ground ginger
1.25 ml (¼ tsp) ground cloves
25 g (1 oz) sugar
15 ml (1 tbsp) malt vinegar
1 small green chilli, deseeded and sliced (optional)

For the parsley and chive sauce
25 g (1 oz) butter
25 g (1 oz) plain flour
300 ml (½ pint) cawl stock and milk mixed
30–45 ml (2–3 tbsp) chopped fresh parsley
15–30 (1–2 tbsp) chopped chives

Wash the joint to remove surface blood. Put the meat into a large clean saucepan and cover well with water. Bring to the boil, then turn the heat down, cover with a lid and simmer for 2 hours. Top up if the water sinks below the level of the meat – at the end of the cooking you should have 1.1 litres (2 pints) of liquor. Leave it to cool, meat and all, and lift off the white hat of grease (it makes good dripping after heating gently to drive off the water). Some families like the fat left in.

Prepare the vegetables – scrub, peel and cut them into bite-sized chunks as appropriate. Wash and slice the leeks into 1 cm (1/2 inch) rings. Then make the sauces.

For the mustard and egg sauce: melt 25 g (1 oz) butter in a small saucepan. When it froths, sprinkle in the flour and cook for a moment until the mixture is sandy. Stir in the mustard powder and turmeric and immediately whisk in the broth and milk. Whisk till the mixture thickens. Chop the egg and stir it in. Finish with the vinegar and beat in the remaining butter. Taste and add salt and pepper.

For the spiced tomato ketchup: put all the ingredients except the optional chilli into a lidded saucepan. Bring to the boil, turn down the heat and leave to simmer gently for 30 minutes. Push the contents of the pan through a sieve. If it's not quite thick enough, return it to the pan and boil it fiercely for a few minutes. Taste and adjust the seasoning. Serve either hot or cold. Finish with a few slices of chilli if you like the ketchup hot.

For the parsley and chive sauce: melt the butter in a small pan, stir in the flour and let it cool for a moment. Whisk in the broth and milk gradually and stir over the heat until the mixture thickens. Mix in the herbs; season.

Reheat the meat in its broth (the *cawl*). Remove the meat and keep it warm while you cook the root vegetables in the broth. Five minutes before you are ready to serve, add the leeks. While the vegetables simmer, boil the potatoes separately. Stir the chopped parsley into the soup just before you bring it to table.

As a second course, serve the meat with the potatoes, and the three sauces.

THE CAWL

The cawl, a clear soup that is the pot-au-feu of Wales, remains very much the usual Welsh family dinner. Traditionally the meat (bacon or beef) is removed from the broth and served with potatoes on the first day. Then the broth is reheated with new vegetables for the second day. On the third day, the vegetables might be strained out and the broth served with thick-cut, buttered bread and cheese.

Welsh Rarebit

Serves 2

225 g (8 oz) grated hard cheese,
    such as Cheddar or Cheshire
1/2 onion, skinned and grated

5 ml (1 tsp) strong mustard
30 ml (2 tbsp) beer
2 slices of toast

Mix together the cheese, grated onion, mustard and beer. Pile the mixture on toast and melt under the grill.

Bara Brith (Speckled Bread)

This is Wales' traditional rich fruit bread. South Wales makes it with baking powder; Northerners prefer yeast as the raising agent. Either way it's delicious.

Makes 1 loaf

175 g (6 oz) dried fruit
225 g (8 oz) dark brown sugar
300 ml (1/2 pint) strong hot tea

275 g (10 oz) self-raising flour
1 egg

Soak the dried fruit and sugar overnight in the tea. You can use either fresh tea, or the cold dregs from the teapot (this gives a good strong colour).

Next day, sift the flour and fold it into the fruit. Mix in the lightly beaten egg. Line a small loaf tin with buttered paper and then tip in the mixture, smoothing it well into the corners.

Bake in the oven at 150°C (300°F) mark 2 for 1 1/2 hours. Cool and store for at least 2 days in a tin so that it matures moist and rich. Traditionalists say you should never butter the Bara Brith, but Dorothy Thomas says *do*, as it's lovely that way.

Welsh Cakes

On sale in every Welsh bakery, these are one of the great delights of teatime. They are easy to make. The Welsh use a flat iron *planc* (a griddle) to bake the cakes, which are cooked on top heat like Scotch pancakes. A heavy frying pan is fine if you don't have a griddle.

Makes 15–18

50 g (2 oz) butter
450 g (1 lb) self-raising flour
100 g (4 oz) sugar

100 g (4 oz) sultanas and raisins
200 ml (7 fl oz) water
2 eggs

Rub the fat into the flour and add the sugar and fruit. Mix the water with the eggs and use to make a soft dough just a little firmer than that for scones. Tip on to a well-floured board and roll out to a thickness of 1 cm (½ inch) Cut out circles with a 6 cm (2½ inch) fluted cutter.

Heat a *planc* or heavy iron frying pan – get the heat up into it gently and thoroughly, and do not let it overheat. If the pan is not well-seasoned or non-stick, slick it with a little butter.

Bake the cakes on the pan, turning them once, until well-risen and lightly browned. They will take about 5 minutes each side.

Sloe Gin

Pennyroyal and valerian used to be included in this cold-weather tipple. It's also lovely made with bullace, damsons or sour cherries. Gather the fruits after the first frost or give them a night in the freezer to soften the skins.

Makes enough to fill a large Kilner jar

450 g (1 lb) sloes
75–100 g (3–4 oz) caster sugar

1 litre (1¾ pints) gin

Prick the sloes all over with a silver needle or fork. Put them into a large Kilner jar with the sugar. Pour in the gin. It will be ready to drink in 3 months, when you should strain it, but is at its best after a year.

Wheat Wine

Makes about 4.5 litres (8 pints)

1.1 litres (2 pints) whole wheat grains
900 g (2 lb) raisins, chopped
1.4 kg (3 lb) demerara sugar
thinly pared rind and juice of
    2 lemons

25 g (1 oz) fresh yeast or 300 ml
    (½ pint) yeast starter

Put the wheat, chopped raisins and sugar into 4.5 litres (8 pints) water with the thinly pared rind and juice of the lemons. Add the yeast or starter. Local author Peggy Cole makes hers with 300 ml (½ pint) warm water frothed with 7.5 ml (1½ tsp) of wine yeast, then she adds 5 ml (1 tsp) of commercial nutrient and 2 Campden tablets (all from the chemist). Cover and leave for 10 days, stirring daily. Strain when all fermentation ceases, then bottle, rack and mature. Wheat wine is at its best if kept for 2 years.

Home-Made Ginger Beer

This home-brew remains a favourite party drink in a Welsh household for both adults and children. You will need eight bottles, or four 1.1 litre (2 pint) bottles. They should be of a strong material and have firm caps with metal springs to imprison the effervescent liquid.

Makes 4.5 litres (8 pints)

50 g (2 oz) fresh ginger or 25 g
    (1 oz) dried
2 lemons
5 ml (1 tsp) cream of tartar

450 g (1 lb) sugar
4.5 litres (8 pints) boiling water
25 g (1 oz) fresh yeast

Roughly crush the ginger root. Wash and slice the lemons into thick rings. Put the ginger, lemon, cream of tartar and sugar in a large bowl. Pour the boiling water over. Stir and leave to cool to blood temperature. Stir in the yeast. Leave to ferment for 24 hours. Skim off the yeast. Strain and bottle the liquid. Leave for 3 days before broaching it.

Tea and Lemon Ice

In all Welsh households the kettle sits permanently on the hob ready to refill the teapot. This delicious ice makes a refreshing change in summer. Or serve it as a dessert with the Welsh cakes, or with a plate of buttered Bara Brith.

Makes about 1.1 litres (2 pints)

300 ml (½ pint) strong fragrant tea
(Lapsang Souchong or Earl
Grey)
2 lemons

225 g (8 oz) sugar
300 ml (½ pint) water
1 egg white
90 ml (6 tbsp) carbonated water

Strain the tea and leave to cool. Peel the lemons, avoiding the bitter pith, and squeeze the juice. Bring the sugar and water to boil with the lemon rind, stirring to dissolve all the sugar. Leave it to cool. Beat the egg white lightly with the carbonated water. Mix all the ingredients thoroughly with a whisk.

Freeze the mixture an ice-cream-maker is best. If you use the ice-making compartment of the fridge, take the ice out when frozen, beat it until it has doubled in volume, and re-freeze. Transfer the ice to the refrigerator 30 minutes before serving.

THE WELL-STOCKED LARDER

'My mother barricaded her larder in times of trouble,' a Hungarian friend explained to me. 'She never locked her street doors, front or back. There was no need for such precautions in a small isolated community where everyone knew everyone else's business. Her money was kept under her mattress in a little kid-skin purse embroidered with bright flowers. The blankets and shawls were kept in a painted wooden chest by the fireplace. We children perched on it to huddle close to the warmth and the cooking-pot in winter. The chest had a little box inside one corner where my mother kept precious spices – I remember pepper and cloves and cinnamon.

'The only door that had a padlock was the door to the larder. In normal times, that was not locked either. It was only in times of war, when the soldiers came – Magyars, Czechs, Turks, Russians, Germans, our own even – that the door was barred with a great iron bolt and the padlock was fixed. Then that larder was barricaded and defended to the death. That is exactly what it meant to my family, that larder; the difference between life and death.'

Europe's peasantry has long been dependent for a healthy diet on a well-stocked storecupboard. In these days of supermarkets and home freezers we forget that until recently the duty of the careful housewife was to spend half the year laying in stores for the other half.

My Scottish grandmother lifted her potatoes in the autumn and carefully stored them in barrels out of the light which would cause them to turn green and sprout. Carrots and turnips were buried in sand-filled boxes, and retrieving them was, to the child I was then, as exciting as a lucky-dip at the local fair. Every autumn she filled the slatted shelves in her loft with perfect rosy apples from her own orchard. It was my job, during the school holidays, to climb into the dark warm rafters and check each apple for the soft brown bruises that could turn all the apples bad. Towards the end of the winter, the quiet air was filled with their wine-scented breath.

In those days a peasant family would share one cooked meal a day. In summer and at harvest time this might well come fresh from the kitchen garden and barnyard. In winter it was a different story: store grains, wheat, barley, oats and rye, and dried vegetables such as beans, peas, and lentils would supply the bulk needed in the cold. Larder stores provided fats and preserved meat and fish, and would make the difference between good and indifferent fare – a bit of home-cured bacon to enhance the flavour, dried mushrooms to enrich the soup, herbs and garlic to perfume the stew.

Today Western Europe still pickles and pots and bakes for the larder, but now it is from choice rather than necessity. The WI markets confirm that Britain's housewives still like to put up their own jams, marmalades and chutneys; the French rural farmer's wife will often salt her own hams and saucisson rather than buying them in the charcuterie; untreated olives are still on sale in the markets of Spain for the locals to brine their own.

Apart from the basic need for fuel food, good cookery is a major item in our vocabulary for expressing affection – be the recipient lover, spouse, child, parent or friend.

A well-stocked larder makes available a vocabulary of love at our fingertips every day, so valuable it is no surprise that it was the one room in the house which needed to be barricaded. The recipes on pages 128–9 are some of my favourite larder stand-bys.

Oriental Salt

Makes 225 g (8 oz)

225 g (8 oz) fine salt	5 ml (1 tsp) freshly ground pepper
5 ml (1 tsp) ground cumin	5 ml (1 tsp) paprika
5 ml (1 tsp) ground coriander	5 ml (1 tsp) cayenne pepper

Mix the salt with the aromatics. Store in a screw-top jar. Oriental salt is the best of accompaniments to wild birds' eggs – particularly gulls' or plovers' eggs and farmed quail eggs. It adds sparkle as well to plain hard-boiled eggs.

Winter Fruit in Brandy

Any dried fruit is delicious macerated and bottled in alcohol (plain *eau-de-vie* is excellent). Raisins are good in an anise-flavoured liquor (*Kümmel* or *Anisette*). Prunes or dried apricots take well to brandy. Soak 700 g (1½ lb) dried fruit in a syrup made with 300 ml (½ pint) water and 225 g (8 oz) sugar. Leave overnight. Next day, bottle the fruit and cover with 1 bottle of the chosen alcohol. It will be ready in a month.

Marinated Winter Fruit

Leave a handful of dried fruit to swell for a few hours in enough orange juice to cover the fruit. Serve the compote with yogurt and a sprinkling of toasted almonds, or with *pain perdu* as a light supper dish.

Sweet-Pickled Cauliflower

This is a favourite Italian pickle for serving as an antipasto. Artichokes, trimmed and sliced, can be prepared in the same fashion. Make double quantities of the pickle and do both at the same time – they are in high season in October.

Makes 1.4 kg (3 lb)

1 large cauliflower, 900 g (2 lb)
    trimmed weight
600 ml (1 pint) boiling water
50 g (2 oz) salt
225 g (8 oz) onions, skinned
600 ml (1 pint) wine vinegar

450 g (1 lb) sugar
15 ml (1 tbsp) mustard seeds
2 short pieces cinnamon stick
2.5 ml ($\frac{1}{2}$ tsp) cloves
2.5 ml ($\frac{1}{2}$ tsp) ground allspice
3 small dried red peppers

Trim the cauliflower and divide it into florets. Blanch the florets in the boiling water with the salt added for 5 minutes. Drain them and rinse under cold running water immediately. Slice the onions and layer them with the cauliflower in sterilised jars.

Heat the vinegar with the sugar and spices, and pour the boiling mixture into the jars. The florets should be submerged. Cover and seal while hot. Ready to eat in a week, the pickle will keep in a cool place all year.

WINTER

There's no doubt that it is in winter that we most appreciate the benefits of the modern life. With light and heat available at the flick of a switch, it's easy to forget that our winter days were once spent ensuring a well-stocked storecupboard, struggling to keep draughty houses warm and the body fuelled with nourishing meals to keep out the cold.

Nevertheless, we still enjoy the hearty traditional dishes of winter – and there's no finer start to a cold day than a proper Scottish breakfast. Set yourself up with a bowl of perfect porridge and cream, followed by a pair of kippers or a smokie – with a choice of shirred oysters or devilled kidneys on the side - and you'll scarcely notice the cold winds of winter.

For some countrydwellers such as Chrissie MacDonald, my neighbour when I lived year-round on Mull, winter meals are still tailored to the requirements of a cold climate. In her cosy little kitchen, the old black range blazes all day and the kettle is always on the hob. For a treat, there's salmon from the sea-loch below her croft-house, maybe lobster from the creels set round the bay, carrageen collected from the shore to set a jelly. A well-made cloutie dumpling is the ceilidh special – and makes the perfect old-fashioned Christmas pudding.

In the south, the Women's Institute has done much to keep our cake-baking skills alive. The WI stalls in any local market are always the first to empty. Fruit cakes and iced sponges, tea-cakes and gingerbreads, load the table at any WI tea.

The highlight of winter remains the great festival of Christmas. Even in the city, our celebrations reflect rural preoccupations. Evergreens, a reminder of the earth's fecundity, are brought in to decorate our houses. We stoke fires and light candles to encourage the returning sun.

But above all, we feast – both as a thanksgiving for harvest past, and as a promise of future plenty. We make merry because we must: winter is a dead season, a season when the earth lies cold and still, and we need to feel the blood coursing through our veins, need to exchange gifts, tell stories, crowd round blazing logs which warm hearts as well as toes, go courting under the mistletoe, raise our glasses to absent friends, and enjoy the excitement of our children.

Anticipation is the soul of celebration – in my family, the build-up to Christmas has become as much of a ritual as the day itself. With my husband and four children, I have spent Christmas in many places. The family favourite remains Provence. Before the festival, the markets are full of game and goose, winter pears and big yellow apples. Our star pleasure is an outing with the neighbour to harvest his truffles. The fragrant tubers do duty as fasting food, taking the place of meat in the Christmas Eve Fasting Supper.

Whether we find ourselves among the rolling vineyards of Provence, in the soft green pastures of Ireland, or snug in the Yorkshire dales, we share the same needs – to gather together and dip into the same pot, to remind each other of the common joys of Christmas past, and above all to enjoy the festival which joins us in hope for the future.

Crofter's Cooking

Chrissie MacDonald's stone-built, two-up, two-down house perches high on a Hebridean hillside. The front garden, rectangular and neatly flower-bedded, gives straight on to the winding single-track road that runs round Mull, the loveliest and most fertile of Scotland's Western Isles. Directly below the road, the life-giving Gulf stream laps the dark rocks and warms the Atlantic-washed shore.

The islanders like to live on the road. All social life courses through this artery. For Chrissie in particular, the road is her life-line. It brings customers, both tourists and locals, for the caravan teashop from which, in the summer season, she sells delicious home baking. The croft's front door is always wide open – rain or shine.

Chrissie does all her cooking in the tiny kitchen tacked on to one end of the house's small living room. Winter and summer, the old black iron range is kept stocked with driftwood and gleanings from the surrounding hazel and birch copses. Here the family gather for their meals – and take advantage of the constant supply of miraculous baking which emerges from Chrissie's ever-busy capacious oven.

Daughters Ann and Alison, and Chrissie's father, the local postmaster until his retirement, share the living room with a steady stream of visitors. A neighbour calls for eggs – the hoodies have been raiding her hen-house again. Chrissie's fisherman brother drops in for a slice of coffee-and-walnut cake and a mug of tea, leaving in return a fistful of small claw-snapping lobsters which have missed the wholesaler.

In Chrissie's grandmother's day, 'puffers', little coastal steamers, would call in once a month at the numerous small harbours round the island and sell the crofters their supplies of flour, sugar and salt. After that, horse-drawn mobile shops toured Mull – although no one needed much in the way of store-bought goods. Most of the necessities of life could be grown, caught or spun. The croft usually supported a cow. Most people smoked their own bacon, and salted their own fish. Wild berries are still gathered for jams and jellies. 'Everyone used to make butter and crowdie – when we were children, crowdie was the usual thing to have in your piece for school.'

Chrissie's cooking remains dependent on the magnificent locally available raw materials. Wild salmon from the rivers, lobsters from the creels which fringe the rocks, Dublin Bay prawns caught inshore – all are served in profusion at weddings and celebrations. For the rest, Chrissie's father likes to salt his own ling, and there is always good fresh herring and mackerel. The family likes a bit of good mutton, well-flavoured from pasturing the upland meadows and perfect for a broth thick with home-grown vegetables and barley.

All this, plus the traditional skill of the Scotswoman with pastry and cakes, means Chrissie's warm, inviting kitchen is never short of appreciative company.

Hebridean Scotch Broth

In this magnificent soup, the barley is the one indispensable ingredient. This can be a two-course soup-stew in the tradition of the *pot-au-feu*, or the meat can be removed and either eaten later with potatoes, or as a cold meat.

Serves 4

700 g (1½ lb) neck of mutton either whole or in chops (use lamb only if you have to)
1.8 litres (3 pints) water
5 ml (1 tsp) salt
75 g (3 oz) barley
1 medium onion
150 g (5 oz) piece of Swedish turnip
1 large or 2 small carrots

1 cm (½ inch) slice off a small white cabbage
1 large leek
black pepper

To finish
60 ml (4 tbsp) chopped fresh parsley

Start to cook this dish the day before serving. Put the neck of mutton in a large saucepan; add the water and salt, cover and simmer lightly for 2 hours (or more if the meat needs it). Skim off all the scum as it rises to the surface.

Take out the meat when it is tender. Put in the barley and leave it soaking in the stock overnight. Next day, bring the stock and barley back to the boil. Prepare and dice all the vegetables quite small. Add all the vegetables except the leek to the stock and cook for 1 hour. Add the leek, cut into fine rings, 10 minutes before the end of the cooking. Season with pepper.

If you want to have the meat in the soup, strip it off the bones, cut it into small pieces and return it to the soup before reheating it thoroughly.

Put a tablespoon of parsley in each of four soup plates, and pour in the soup.

If you prefer a two-dish meal, serve the meat as a main course afterwards with potatoes – Golden Wonder are Chrissie's preferred variety. Bake the potatoes if they are mature. Or boil them in their jackets if they are new. For really fluffy, floury boiled potatoes, Chrissie cooks hers whole and unpeeled (never cut a Golden Wonder) for 12–15 minutes, depending on the size. Then drain out all but a little of the water, lid the pan tightly and *steam* the potatoes for another 10–15 minutes, shaking regularly, until they are dry and floury in texture.

Skirlie with Mushrooms

Skirlie is only worth making with good drippings from roasted meat. Chrissie MacDonald recalls that sometimes the cook at the big house would dole out, to people who wanted it, the wonderful rich dripping that had been used for umpteen big roasts. I like skirlie as a kind of risotto, made with wild chanterelles that grow in profusion all over the island.

Serves 4

225 g (8 oz) mushrooms (wild if available)
150 g (5 oz) good meat dripping

2 medium onions, skinned and thinly sliced
450 g (1 lb) medium oatmeal
salt and black pepper

Wipe and slice the mushrooms. Fry them in 25 g (1 oz) of dripping in a large frying pan. Remove them and reserve. Heat the rest of the dripping. Fry the onions. When the onions are soft but not brown, turn up the heat.

Add the oatmeal, turn it in the dripping and brown it a bit. Return the mushrooms to the pan. Add salt and pepper to taste. Serve hot.

Crowdie Butter

This is not the usual oat gruel, but a fresh white cheese, naturally soured, or turned with rennet. It needs a little livening with herbs – or spark it up with wild garlic.

Makes 150–175 g (5–6 oz)

1.1 litres (2 pints) full cream milk
10 ml (2 tsp) rennet (or follow instructions on the packet)
2.5 ml ($\frac{1}{2}$ tsp) salt
black pepper

1 garlic clove, skinned
15 ml (1 tbsp) chopped fresh parsley
50 g (2 oz) butter

Heat the milk to 40°C (100°F). Stir in the rennet. Leave in a warm place until the milk junkets. Line a sieve with muslin wrung out in boiling water. Place over a bowl, tip in the junket and let it drain until crumbly. Work in the salt and pepper, garlic, chopped parsley and butter.

Highland Oatcakes

Oatcakes baked on a black iron girdle suspended over the top heat of the fire were the basic bread of the Highlands and Islands. There was a special rack to dry the cakes after cooking, which gave them the characteristic 'curl to the fire'.

Serves 4

225 g (8 oz) medium oatmeal
5 ml (1 tsp) salt

45–60 ml (3–4 tbsp) hot water
15 g (½ oz) dripping or lard

Sift oatmeal and salt into a large bowl. Put on the girdle or in a heavy frying pan to heat. Bring the water to the boil with the fat. Pour into a well in the oatmeal. Work into a stiff dough and cut in half. Roll out on a floured board to the size of a dinner plate and about 3 mm (⅛ inch) thick. Cut into quarters or farles. Repeat with the remaining dough.

Test the girdle's heat by holding your hand over it. Lay on one of the quartered rounds. When the farles are ready, the surface stops steaming and begins to look dry and white. Turn the farle over and cook the other side. Repeat with the other farles. Dry off the oatcakes and lightly brown the edges in a hot oven or under the grill.

Lobster Tart

Chrissie's pastry is famous. Her nimble fingers can make a feather-light pastry from a half-fat-to-flour mix. The rest of us can improve our chances of success by increasing the fat.

Serves 4

For the pastry
225 g (8 oz) plain flour
pinch of salt
75 g (3 oz) cold lard

75 g (3 oz) cold butter
45–60 ml (3–4 tbsp) ice-cold water

For the filling

One live lobster – and it should be good and lively. A 'cripple' – that is, one with only one claw for which you should pay less – will do fine for this dish.	**5 egg yolks**
	4 egg whites
	300 ml (¹/₂ pint) milk
	300 ml (¹/₂ pint) single cream
	salt and pepper

M ake the pastry first. Sift the flour with the salt into a large bowl. Chop the lard and butter into the flour with a sharp knife. Finish rubbing in the fat to flour with the tips of your fingers. Work in enough ice-cold water to give you a ball of soft (but not sticky) dough. Cover with cling-film and leave the dough to rest in a cool place for about 30 minutes.

Bring a large saucepan of salted water to the boil – enough to cover the lobster. Kill the lobster (or have your fishmonger do so) with a knife slipped in behind its head. Or plunge the creature in the boiling water and hold it under with a wooden spoon.

Cook the lobster for 3–4 minutes – just long enough to turn the shell scarlet and make the lobster easier to skin. Drain it, sever the head and cut it in half, taking care to save the greenish black brain (rather like liquid seaweed). This will turn anything into which it is stirred a wonderful sunny scarlet as it cooks. Reserve the brain for making lobster butter (see Salmon with Lobster Butter, page 139). Otherwise, it can go into the tart filling.

Remove the lobster meat from the body, claws and head (leave out the dark intestine which runs right down the body, and the stomach at the top of the head). Slice the body meat into medallions. Leave the claw meat whole.

Roll out the pastry as thinly as possible on a cold floured surface and use to line a tart tin. Line the pastry with greaseproof paper and weight it down with dried beans. Bake in the oven at 190°C (375°F) mark 5 for 10 minutes. Remove beans and paper.

Beat the egg yolks and whites, milk, and cream together and season. Pour the mixture into the cooled tart tin. Arrange the lobster pieces over the top. Bake at 200°C (400°F) mark 6 for 30 minutes until the filling is set.

Wild Herb Tart

In the Hebrides, storms can barricade the harbours for weeks, so no fisherman can get out to his creels. Instead of a lobster, make this delicious fresh-flavoured herb tart. Chrissie herself does not use wild greens, apart from watercress, in her own cooking. But as a child she used to eat her way to school and back, nibbling a variety of leaves – sorrel, clover stalks, cress, or a bit of turnip top snatched from the field.

Serves 4

1 quantity of pastry (see Lobster
   Tart, above)
50 g (2 oz) fresh leaf spinach
50 g (2 oz) sorrel, dandelion, nettle
   tops and/or watercress
1 large leek
3–4 spring onions
60–90 ml (4–6 tbsp) chopped fresh
   parsley

5 egg yolks
4 egg whites
300 ml (½ pint) milk
300 ml (½ pint) single cream
salt and pepper
75 g (3 oz) cheese, grated (Scottish
   Cheddar is excellent)

Make the tart as in the recipe above, replacing the lobster with the greens, washed and shredded, but not cooked. Stir in the cheese before baking.

Salmon with Lobster Butter

Salmon is Chrissie's favourite dish for special occasions. A freshly caught salmon has a white curd in between the tender pink flakes of flesh. The lobster butter is a party version of the melted butter which the islanders use to sauce their salt fish.

Serves 10–12

1 whole 3.2–3.6 kg (7–8 lb) salmon
salt

For the butter
juice of 1/2 lemon
175 g (6 oz) cold butter, cut into
  pieces

green-black brain from the head of
  a lobster, or 45–60 ml (3–4 tbsp)
  heavily reduced lobster stock
  (made from shells and heads)

Scale, gut and wipe the fish. Rub inside the cavity with salt. If you have a fish kettle, steam the salmon whole over boiling water for 30–35 minutes (making sure the water is kept topped up). Or wrap the fish in lightly oiled foil and bake it in the oven at 170°C (325°F) mark 3 for 1 hour. Leave the fish to rest while you make the butter.

Warm the lemon juice in a small bowl set over a saucepan of simmering water. Beat in the nuggets of cold butter, adding more as each one melts. Do this gently – it can split if you over-heat it (revive it with a quick splash of cold water if this does happen). When you have a smooth sauce like thin cream, sieve and whisk in the greenish black brain of the lobster – which immediately turns the butter a wonderful orange-pink.

Serve the salmon when it is just cool but still sweet-flavoured and full of its own juices, with hot baked potatoes and warm lobster butter.

Carrageen Pudding with Rhubarb Jelly

Carrageen is a purple-brown or green fronded seaweed common on Scottish beaches on the mid-tide line. It can be used to set and delicately flavour a jelly or thicken a soup. If you gather carrageen fresh, you will need 50 g (2 oz) to set 600 ml (1 pint) of milk. Dried carrageen is available in health-food stores, or Chinese supermarkets in processed form, as agar-agar.

Serves 4

900 ml (1½ pints) milk	1 egg
1 strip lemon rind	2 sticks rhubarb, sliced and lightly
15 g (½ oz) prepared dried	poached with sugar
carrageen	60 ml (4 tbsp) rosehip or redcurrant
15 ml (1 tbsp) sugar	jelly

Bring the milk to the boil with the lemon rind. Stir in the carrageen and cook for about 2 minutes until the milk thickens enough to coat the back of a wooden spoon. Add the sugar.

Allow the mixture to cool until it is at blood temperature, 40°C (100°F). Whisk the egg until frothy and then whisk in the warm milk until smooth. Pour the mixture through a sieve into a cold, wetted ring-mould. Then put it in the refrigerator to set – it will only take about 30 minutes.

Run hot water over the outside of the mould and turn out the jelly. Fill the middle of the ring with a ladleful of rhubarb compote and surround with some scarlet sauce made of rosehip or redcurrant jelly melted in a little hot water.

Cloutie Dumpling and Ginger Sauce

Chrissie's family likes its cloutie dumpling served cold as a fruit-cake (a favourite treat for birthdays, picnics and special occasions). Some people like to serve the cloutie dumpling hot with custard. I like it with ginger sauce.

Serves 8

For the dumpling
450 g (1 lb) self-raising flour
175 g (6 oz) soft fresh brown breadcrumbs
100 g (4 oz) soft brown sugar
5 ml (1 tsp) mixed spice
pinch of ground cinnamon
225 g (8 oz) currants
225 g (8 oz) sultanas
150 g (5 oz) butter or vegetable fat
15 ml (1 tbsp) black treacle

1 egg
150 ml (¼ pint) milk
2 grated apples, cored but not peeled
1 mature carrot, grated

For the ginger sauce
1 wine glass Crabbe's Green Ginger Wine
3 egg yolks
150 ml (¼ pint) single cream

Sift the flour and mix it with the breadcrumbs, brown sugar and spices. Mix in the currants and sultanas. Melt the butter or vegetable fat gently with the treacle. Beat the egg and milk together and add to the dry ingredients, with the grated apples and carrot – use your hands to mix. Stir in the butter and treacle mixture. Add more milk if necessary to give a soft mixture which drops easily from the spoon.

Scald a 45 cm (18 inch) square of cotton sheet in a large saucepan of boiling water with an upturned plate on the bottom. Take out the scalded cloth, sprinkle it with flour and put the dumpling into it. Draw up the edges, and tie up firmly with white string, leaving enough room for the pudding to expand. Lower the dumpling back into the boiling water. Bring back to the boil, then boil steadily but gently for 4 hours. It can be longer but it shouldn't be less. Top up the water as necessary.

Remove the dumpling and dip it straight in and out of cold water. Unwrap the dumpling on to a serving plate. The skin will initially be white from the flour. Put it on the plate in a very low oven to dry off for 20 minutes – it will develop a fine, dark glossy skin.

Meanwhile, make the ginger sauce. Beat the wine with the egg yolks over hot water until the mixture is thick, white and fluffy. Stir in the cream. Serve the sauce in a pretty glass jug, with the hot pudding.

The dumpling cuts wonderfully rich and dark. Leftover slices are delicious fried in butter and served with cream for a teatime treat.

Winter Breakfasts

Among the several tribes that inhabit our islands, none breakfast better than the Scots. While the rest of the world breaks its fast with a cup and a crust, and thinks about something more substantial around 10 or 11 o'clock, the Scots do otherwise.

Indeed, in the old days they breakfasted to such good effect that the English complained, with some justification, that it was the Scots' habit of breaking their fast on a fortifying bowl of porridge that won them the battle of Bannockburn. Robert the Bruce might have had a small hand in it; nevertheless, where the English could manage only one mile, the Scots marched for 10 across the heather on nothing more than a diet of oats dipped in water.

One place that has long been known for the quality of its breakfasts is The Creggans Inn, a small family hotel on the southern shore of Loch Fyne, run by Veronica and Fitzroy Maclean with their son, Charlie. And it is Lady Maclean, whose 1965 book *Lady Maclean's Cook Book* is still in use in many country-house kitchens up and down the land, who sees to that.

The most powerful influence in the kitchen, after Lady Maclean herself, is Jimmie MacNab. Officially, Jimmie is the breakfast and game cook, in charge of porridge, Loch Fyne kippers, black pudding and sausages. Unofficially, for 14 years Jimmie has been the sergeant-major of the whole establishment, intercepting local supplies of lobster and baby scallops, turbot and wild salmon, halibut and oysters before they are whisked away to some distant hotel or restaurant. Seated majestically at his scrubbed wooden table at the end of the kitchen, he directs breakfast with aplomb. And his skill at oyster-opening, porridge-brewing and kedgeree-making is as legendary as his waistline.

Breakfast Kedgeree

This dish is a legacy from the British Raj, where it was made with lentils and rice. It can be prepared the night before and warmed up in a gentle oven in the morning. Make it with Arbroath smokies or, even more luxurious, trimmings of smoked salmon.

Serves 4

225 g (8 oz) long-grain rice
225 g (8 oz) smoked haddock
a little milk
4 eggs
2–3 spring onions, chopped

300 ml (½ pint) single cream
salt and pepper
50–75 g (2–3 oz) butter
15 ml (1 tbsp) chopped fresh
   parsley

Boil the rice until it is dry and fluffy. Meanwhile, poach the haddock in a little milk, then drain, skin, debone and flake it.

Boil the eggs until they are hard, but do not over-boil, which makes the yolk go green at the edges. For the best results, put them into warm water and bring to the boil. Turn down the heat and simmer for 5–6 minutes, depending on size. Put them straight into cold water to loosen the shells. Shell them as soon as they are cool enough to handle. Reserve 2 yolks as garnish and finely chop the rest.

Toss the fish with the rice and chopped eggs, then mix in the chopped spring onions and cream and season with salt and pepper.

Spread the kedgeree in an ovenproof dish, dot with four knobs of butter, cover with foil and bake in the oven at 180°C (350°F) mark 4 for 20–30 minutes. Garnish with the chopped reserved yolk and the chopped parsley.

Jugged Smokies

Arbroath smokies are smoked haddock with their heads removed, but ungutted so that the flavour is gamier. To reheat the fish, pop them in a jug, tails uppermost and still tied together in pairs, then fill the jug with boiling water. Leave the jug on the side of the stove for 20–30 minutes until the smokies are warmed through. Serve them on a warm plate with a knob of butter. You can heat kippers in the same way; they will need about 5 minutes.

Eggs in Black Butter

This is one of Lady Maclean's favourites.

First, trim the crusts from a slice of white bread to make a rough circle, and set aside. In a frying pan, brown a good knob of butter and add a tablespoon of Worcester sauce and some lemon juice until the mixture tastes sharp. Put a biscuit-cutting ring into the pan and fry an egg inside it. Remove the egg, fry the bread round in the butter and serve the egg on its fried base, with the remaining black butter poured over.

Kidneys with Bacon

For two people, halve 3 kidneys, core and wrap in very finely cut streaky bacon – pancetta, available from Italian delicatessens and some supermarkets, is the best. Grill them on a flat baking tray so that you don't lose the juices.

Jimmie's Porridge

Serve this in a wooden bowl and eat it with a deerhorn spoon, dipping each spoonful into the cream bowl before you eat the porridge. This isn't just folklore; having taken the trouble to heat the porridge, you don't want it to cool down before you've finished, which is what happens if you pour cream into it. 'You have to teach an Englishman how to eat his porridge,' Jimmie laughs. 'I like plenty of salt in mine – no sugar.' Each teacup holds about 200 ml (7 fl oz). Quantities can be varied as long as you follow the same proportions.

Serves 4

2 teacups fine oatmeal
½ teacup pinhead oatmeal (or
   whole oats roughly chopped in
   a coffee grinder)

6 teacups water
salt
cream

Put the oatmeal to soak in the water overnight in a saucepan. Bring the mixture to the boil, turn down the heat and let it simmer gently, uncovered, for 20–30 minutes. Stir it regularly until it is ready to serve. Add salt to taste and serve with a bowl of cream on the side.

Hatted Oysters

This is Jimmie MacNab's special recipe. The oysters come from John Noble at nearby Ardkinglass. Since the oysters are to be cooked anyway, pop them in a hot oven for a minute or two to open.

Serves 2–3 as a starter

12 oysters on the half shell
45–60 ml (3–4 tbsp) toasted brown
   breadcrumbs
30 ml (2 tbsp) finely chopped fresh
   parsley

1 garlic clove, skinned and finely
   chopped
50 g (2 oz) butter
black pepper
lemon quarters

Top each oyster with a sprinkle of breadcrumbs, parsley and garlic. Dot with a tiny knob of butter and finish with black pepper.

Toast under a hot grill for 2–3 minutes – the oyster should only just be warmed, but the hat must be crisp and sizzling. Serve with lemon quarters.

Shirred Oysters

This is Veronica Maclean's recipe from Richmond, Virginia, as prepared by Mrs Fitzgerald Beamiss, a member of the FFV – First Families of Virginia. It's the Christmas special.

Shuck the oysters and tip the liquor into a frying pan with a good helping of double cream. Bring to the boil and slip in the oysters for 1½ minutes until they curl. Serve with thin slivers of peach-glazed Virginia ham, prosciutto or any other good ham.

Herrings with Mustard Cream

When choosing your herrings, look for really fresh fish, slate-grey in colour with very light pink bellies, bright eyes and scarlet gills. They should not be too red on the head.

Serves 4

4 split and boned herrings
salt and pepper
1 small egg beaten with 15 ml
    (1 tbsp) milk
pinhead oatmeal (or whole oats
    roughly chopped in a coffee
    grinder)

For the mustard cream
150 ml (1/4 pint) whipping cream
15 ml (1 tbsp) mustard

Gut and debone the herrings. This is easy to do if you run your thumb through the belly, up one side of the backbone, then down the other side. Pull off the head, bringing the backbone with it. Season the herrings, then coat with the egg and milk mixture and press them firmly into the oatmeal.

Grill the fish, turning once. Herrings are fatty enough to baste themselves, but you could fry them if you prefer.

Whip the cream lightly, fold in the mustard and serve with the herrings.

Variation Trout are also good prepared in this way, but mix grated horseradish into the cream in place of the mustard.

Salmon Fishcakes

This is the Macleans' housekeeper's recipe, and a family favourite. The fishcakes can be frozen after breadcrumbing, if wished.

Serves 4

900 g (2 lb) potatoes
225 g (8 oz) salmon tail
5 ml (1 tsp) anchovy essence
salt and pepper

60 ml (4 tbsp) seasoned flour
1 egg beaten with 45 ml (3 tbsp) milk
120 ml (8 tbsp) fresh breadcrumbs
vegetable oil for frying

Boil, skin and mash the potatoes. Poach the salmon by putting it on top of them for the last 10 minutes of cooking, then flake and mix it with the mash.

Season with anchovy essence, salt and pepper. Form the mixture into patties and leave them until cool and firm.

Set out three plates in a line, with seasoned flour in one, egg and milk in the next, and breadcrumbs in the last. Dust the fishcakes through the flour, dip them in egg and milk, and then press them firmly in the breadcrumbs. Fry in shallow oil until the fishcakes are golden, turning once.

Soda Scones

Also called girdle cakes, these deserve that name only if they have the characteristic flat top and bottom that indicates they have been cooked on a girdle. Scones belong to the tradition of top-heat unleavened breads made without yeast.

Makes 4 scones

175 g (6 oz) plain flour
4 ml (3/4 tsp) cream of tartar
2.5 ml (1/2 tsp) bicarbonate of soda

15 ml (1 tbsp) caster sugar
60–75 ml (4–5 tbsp) milk

Mix the dry ingredients together with enough milk to make a soft dough. Shape into a round and press out with the heel of your hand to a 15 cm (6 inch) diameter.

Cut into quarters and cook over a medium heat either on the girdle or in a heavy frying pan, very lightly greased, with oil, for about 15 minutes until nicely browned and the centre of the scone is cooked. Turn the scone over and cook the other side.

Scotch Pancakes

Also known as drop scones, these are made with an egg-enriched mix – wet enough to drop from the spoon, but lightened with bicarbonate of soda.

Makes 15–20 pancakes

225 g (8 oz) self-raising flour
10 ml (2 tsp) bicarbonate of soda
75 g (3 oz) caster sugar

2 eggs
30 ml (2 tbsp) vegetable oil
scant 300 ml (½ pint) milk

Mix all the ingredients together – this is easiest in a blender. Grease a girdle or heavy frying pan once only. When it is very hot, turn the heat down and drop tablespoons of the mixture on to the hot surface. It will brown underneath (don't let it cook too fast or it will burn) and bubble on top. When the top bubbles have burst, turn the pancakes over and cook the other side. Repeat until all the mixture is used.

Britain's biggest organisation for countrywomen was found- # Baking with the WI

ed in the First World War when WI members' efforts helped to feed the nation. While it quickly became a forum and campaigning pressure group, concerned with everything from toxic waste and deforestation to the introduction of food irradiation, the early emphasis on home cooking has remained at the heart of village activity.

It was jam – plum jam in particular – which earned the WIs their special place in our national affections during both World Wars. Their jam-making campaign soon became a national government-sponsored effort, with 2,600 jam-making centres at work.

The most visible activity of the WI is its markets – sometimes only a stall or two set up on market day in the local town, where the early bird catches the worm. Here can be bought the best of local baking; and preserves and chutney, made by the most expert hands in the village, are available in due season – strawberry jam in summer, plum jam in autumn, lemon curd and marmalade in winter, with mincemeat at Christmas time. Sometimes there is local honey, lovely little bantam eggs (for the nicest Scotch eggs), duck eggs with pale-blue translucent whites for cakes and custard. All year round, too, the Village Produce Associations make sure of good fresh vegetables, herbs, potted plants and seasonal fruit.

And the WI market is the perfect place to find regional specialities: Cumberland rum·butter in its native territory, home-made clotted cream down in Cornwall. The success of the markets – today they generate more than £8 million worth of business a year – and the Village Produce Associations which supply them, lies at the heart of the whole WI movement. The first WI market was held within a year of the first WI meeting, in response to war-time difficulties in food distribution.

Still comfortably rooted in its rural membership, the WI has adapted to the population shifts of the post-war years. In 1965 the NFWI, recognising the changes in work patterns which had created large semi-urban populations, altered its constitutional rules against recruiting in communities numbering more than 4,000. County chairman Mrs Frances Charlton immediately took the proffered opportunity: 'We went into the housing estates looking for members. I remember forming a WI in the west end of Newcastle. We got them all to wear a label with the name and address and you saw them looking at the labels and saying, "You live in our street and you only live three doors away from me." I think opening a WI did a tremendous amount for the people living on those estates.'

The village of Collingham in Nottinghamshire has seen many a change since it was established in Saxon times. It has a new housing estate, and the Inter-city train to London has brought young commuters in search of affordable homes. The Collingham WI uses its great energies to draw them all into village life, to pass on their traditional skills, and to share news and argue views – from the effects of chemicals on food to the Keep Britain Tidy campaign.

Sausage Plait

This sausage plait is made with a lovely flaky lard pastry.

Serves 4

For the pastry
200 g (7 oz) plain flour
5 ml (1 tsp) salt
150 g (5 oz) lard
30–45 ml (2–3 tbsp) ice-cold water

For the filling
15 g (½ oz) lard
1 medium onion, skinned and
   chopped

5 ml (1 tsp) dried thyme
2.5 ml (½ tsp) dried sage (sage is
   very powerful)
salt and pepper
350 g (12 oz) sausagemeat
15 ml (1 tbsp) beaten egg

Sift the flour and salt into a bowl. Cut the fat roughly into the flour, using a sharp knife. Cut in the water, until you have a firm but soft dough, worked together at the end with the tips of your fingers. Leave the dough to rest for 15–20 minutes, while you make the filling.

Melt the 15 g (½ oz) lard in a small saucepan, and fry the chopped onion until it is soft. Work the cooked onion, herbs and seasonings into the sausagemeat until they are well mixed. On a floured board, roll out the rested pastry into a 25 cm (10 inch) square.

Lay the sausagemeat in a 7.5 cm (3 inch) wide ribbon down the middle of the square, leaving a finger-wide margin at either end. Slash the two long sides of the pastry seven times diagonally towards the filling. Dampen the edges of the pastry. Fold each end over the sausagemeat, and then fold over the long sides, overlapping the cut pieces to give a plaited effect. Paint with beaten egg for a shiny glaze.

Bake in the oven at 200°C (400°F) mark 6 for 40 minutes until the pastry is crisp and golden, and the sausage is cooked through.

Lincolnshire Chine

This bacon recipe from over the border has long been a popular party dish in Collingham in Nottinghamshire. In the 1920s, a correspondent of Florence White's English Folk Cookery Association supplied a definition. 'This christening or fore-chine was cut down each side of the backbone of a pig and it was so called because one was generally saved for a christening.'

Serves 6–8

1.4 kg (3 lb) joint shoulder bacon, boned

1.1 litres (2 pints) parsley, roughly chopped

60 ml (4 tbsp) chopped chives or leek tops

30 ml (2 tbsp) roughly chopped fresh marjoram

5 ml (1 tsp) ground mace

Soak the bacon overnight if your butcher thinks it necessary. Lay the joint skin-side down on a board and cut deep slits 1 cm (1/2 inch) apart in the meat, taking care not to cut through the skin.

Stuff the cuts with the herbs and spice, which have been mixed together – a food processor does the job beautifully. Tie the joint up neatly, and put it in a boiling bag in a large saucepanful of cold water. Bring it to the boil, turn down the heat, and boil steadily for 1 hour from the time the water has boiled.

Let the joint cool in the bag in its own juices and serve it cold: it is perfect with a slice of Cottage Loaf (see page 154).

Plum Jam

Here is the jam which started it all.

Makes 2.8 kg (6 lb)

1.8 kg (4 lb) plums   **. 1.8 kg (4 lb) sugar**
water

Stone the plums and crack a few stones for the kernels to add to the jam. Put the plums to boil, with enough water to cover them, in a large saucepan or preserving pan. When they are soft, about 20 minutes, weigh the pulp and allow 450 g (1 lb) sugar to 450 g (1 lb) fruit.

Put the sugar in the pan with enough water to allow the granules to melt. Bring gently to the boil, stirring until the sugar dissolves. Stir in the fruit and the kernels. Boil for 20–30 minutes, stirring, until the jam is thick and a test dab sets on a cold saucer.

Pot in sterilised jars.

Lemon Curd

Makes about 700 g (1¹/₂ lb)

4 lemons   **100 g (4 oz) butter, chopped into**
350 g (12 oz) granulated or   **small cubes**
preserving sugar   **4 egg yolks**

Wash the lemons and grate the peel finely. Squeeze the juice and strain it into a bowl with the grated peel, sugar and butter.

Set the bowl over a saucepan of simmering water and leave the ingredients to dissolve together gently.

Fork the egg yolks together and strain them. Whisk in the lemon mixture. Return the mixture to the bowl over the simmering water and whisk as the mixture cooks and thickens. Don't let it boil.

When the curd has a slightly jellied thickened look, it is done. This will take 20–30 minutes. It will thicken further as it cools and the butter solidifies. Pot in sterilised jars. Store in the refrigerator.

Cottage Loaves

This is Edith Hawkin's (one-time President of Collingham's Produce Association) standard bread recipe.

Makes 3 brown cottage loaves

1.4 kg (3 lb) wholemeal flour (with a little handful of white to lighten it)	100 g (4 oz) fresh yeast or 50 g (2 oz) dried
5 ml (1 tsp) salt	5 ml (1 tsp) sugar
	600 ml (1 pint) warm water

Put the flour and salt in a bowl and make a hollow in the centre. Cream the yeast with the sugar and mix in a cup of the warm water. Pour into the hollow and let it froth. Work it, and the rest of the water, in with a fork.

When the dough is well mixed, knead it, adding more flour if necessary, until you have a nice soft dough. Put it to rise in a warm place in a bowl covered with a clean cloth. When it fills the mixing bowl (in an hour or so), knock it down and cut it into four pieces. Cut one of the pieces into three and knead each piece into a ball. Knead the three large pieces into round loaves, knuckle a hole in the middle and put a small ball on top. Put the loaves back in a warm place to double in size.

Bake them in the oven at 190°C (375°F) mark 5 for 30 minutes until they are well risen, and hollow when you tap them on the base. Transfer to wire racks to cool.

Harvo Bread

A tried-and-tested cut-and-come-again cake. The combination of boiling and baking, and the measurements in cups (use a 300 ml (½ pint) coffee mug), confirms its venerable pedigree.

Makes 1 loaf

3 cups plain flour	1 egg, lightly beaten
5 ml (1 tsp) bicarbonate of soda	1 cup water
1 cup caster sugar	50 g (2 oz) margarine
225 g (8 oz) sultanas or raisins	30 ml (2 tbsp) golden syrup

Mix together the flour sifted with the bicarbonate of soda, sugar and fruit. Stir in the egg. Heat the water with the margarine and the syrup until all is melted. Stir the mixture thoroughly into the rest of the ingredients.

Grease a medium-sized loaf tin and line the base with greaseproof paper. Spoon in the cake ingredients. Bake in the oven at 170°C (325°F) mark 3 for about 1³/₄ hours until well risen.

Borrowdale Tea Bread

This rich fruit bread comes from Borrowdale in Cumbria.

Makes 1 long loaf

450 g (1 lb) mixed fruit, soaked
  overnight in 450 ml (³/₄ pint) tea
250 g (9 oz) stoneground wholemeal
  flour

5 ml (1 tsp) bicarbonate of soda
175 g (6 oz) brown sugar
25 g (1 oz) butter, melted
1 egg

Mix all the ingredients together thoroughly, including any unabsorbed tea, adding them in the order given. Butter and line a long loaf tin with greaseproof paper. Tip in the mixture and spread it evenly.

Bake in the oven at 170°C (325°F) mark 3 for 1¹/₂ hours, until firm and a nkewer inserted into the centre comes out clean. Cool on a wire rack.

Caldbeck Gingerbread

This recipe comes from the energetic branch of the WI in Caldbeck, Cumbria. It is made with a mixture of wholemeal and soya flour, with sunflower and sesame seeds thrown in.

Makes about 18 pieces

75 g (3 oz) butter
75 g (3 oz) lard
350 g (12 oz) wholemeal flour
100 g (4 oz) soya flour
50 g (2 oz) sesame seeds
50 g (2 oz) sunflower seeds,

roughly crushed

5 ml (1 tsp) bicarbonate of soda
2.5 ml (¹/₂ tsp) salt
175 g (6 oz) brown sugar
30 ml (2 tsp) black treacle
7.5 ml (1¹/₂ tsp) ground ginger

Cream together the butter and lard, then knead all the ingredients to a stiff dough with your hands (or in a mixer). Roll or press out the dough and lay it in a buttered 30 x 23 cm (12 x 9 inch) Swiss-roll tin or roasting tin.

Bake the gingerbread in the oven at 180*C (350*F) mark 4 for about 45 minutes until firm and well-risen. Cut it into roughly 6 cm (2¹/₂ inch) squares and transfer the pieces to a wire rack to cool.

Coffee and Walnut Cake

Makes 1 cake

For the cake
225 g (8 oz) sugar
225 g (8 oz) margarine
4 eggs
225 g (8 oz) self-raising flour
10 ml (2 tsp) instant coffee dissolved
   in 30 ml (2 tbsp) hot water
50 g (2 oz) walnut pieces

For the icing
75 g (3 oz) soft margarine
350 g (12 oz) icing sugar
15 ml (1 tbsp) instant coffee
   dissolved in 45 ml (3 tbsp) hot
   water
8–9 whole walnuts

Make the cake: cream the sugar with the margarine until light and fluffy. Beat in the eggs and fold in the flour, coffee and walnut pieces.

Butter two 20 cm (8 inch) diameter cake tins and divide the mixture between them. Bake in the oven at 180°C (350°F) mark 4 for 20–25 minutes until nicely risen and spongy to the finger. Turn the cakes out on to a wire rack and leave to cool.

Make the icing: beat the margarine with the icing sugar, adding the coffee and, if necessary, enough extra water to give a soft but firm icing.

Sandwich the cooled cakes together with one third of the icing. Spread the rest over the top and sides. Decorate with whole walnuts.

Chocolate Cake

Ruth Pegg acquired her baking skills in domestic science classes at school, and remembers being instructed to beat the mixture for this cake with her hand – the warmth creamed the hard margarine beautifully.

Makes 1 cake

For the cake
200 g (7 oz) self-raising flour
25 g (1 oz) cocoa powder
225 g (8 oz) sugar
100 g (4 oz) margarine
2 eggs
75 ml (5 tbsp) evaporated milk
75 ml (5 tbsp) cold water

For the icing
65 g (2½ oz) softened margarine
60 ml (4 tbsp) cocoa powder
225 g (8 oz) icing sugar
45 ml (3 tbsp) milk

Make the cake: mix together the flour, cocoa and sugar. Cut the margarine into the mixture and finish by rubbing it in thoroughly with your fingertips. Stir in the 2 eggs forked up with the evaporated milk and cold water.

Butter two 20 cm (8 inch) round cake tins and divide the mixture between them. Bake in the oven at 180°C (350°F) mark 4 for 30–35 minutes until the cakes feel firm to your finger. Turn them out immediately on to a wire rack to cool.

Make the icing: cream the margarine with the cocoa, icing sugar and milk. Sandwich the cooled cakes together with half the icing. Spread the rest over the top.

Carrot Cake

Many of the old country recipes make use of the natural sweetness of vegetables – particularly carrots and parsnips – in puddings and cakes. During the war, people returned to these habits of economy from sheer necessity.

Makes 1 cake

For the cake
175 g (6 oz) wholemeal flour
10 ml (2 tsp) baking powder
pinch of salt
5 ml (1 tsp) ground cinnamon
100 g (4 oz) margarine
100 g (4 oz) brown sugar
100 g (4 oz) grated carrot

grated rind of 1/2 orange
2 large eggs
15 ml (1 tbsp) milk

For the icing
100 g (4 oz) soft white cheese
clear honey
a few walnut pieces

Make the cake: sift the flour with the baking powder, salt and cinnamon. Beat the margarine with the sugar, then stir in the grated carrot and orange rind. Beat in the eggs, lightly forked with the milk. Fold in the flour mixture.

Butter two 15 cm (6 inch) round cake tins and divide the cake mixture between them.

Bake in the oven at 170°C (325°F) mark 3 for 45–60 minutes until firm and well browned. Allow the cakes to settle in the tins for a moment, then turn them out on to a wire rack to cool.

Make the icing: mix the soft white cheese with the honey. Sandwich the cakes together with half the mixture, and top with the other half. Decorate with walnut pieces.

Cumberland Rum Nicky

The cooks of Cumbria have a sure hand with the spices. This strength is reflected in sweet specialities such as a nicky. Everyone in Cumbria has a family recipe for this double-crust ginger-spiced mincemeat tart that is flavoured with the rum and the spices supplied, in the old days, via the Atlantic trade ports of Whitehaven, Maryport and Silloth. Until recently it was still made with beef marrow. Start a day ahead: the fruit has to be soaked.

Serves 4–6

For the filling
225 g (8 oz) dates, chopped
100 g (4 oz) raisins
100 g (4 oz) currants
15 ml (1 tbsp) crystallised stem ginger, chopped small
1 wine glass dark rum
1 large Bramley apple, peeled, cored and chopped small
50 g (2 oz) butter, softened
50 g (2 oz) soft brown sugar

For the pastry
225 g (8 oz) plain flour
salt
75 g (3 oz) butter
75 g (3 oz) lard
60–75 ml (4–5 tbsp) ice-cold water

To finish
15 ml (1 tbsp) milk
15 ml (1 tbsp) unrefined granulated sugar

Put the dates, raisins, currants and ginger to soak overnight in the rum in a covered bowl.

Next day, make the pastry first. Make sure all ingredients are cold. Sift the flour with the salt into a bowl. Using your fingertips, rub the fat into the flour until you have a mixture like fine breadcrumbs. Work in enough cold water to give a soft dough.

Leave the dough to rest under cover in a cool larder or the refrigerator for 30 minutes. Mix the rest of the filling ingredients with the soaked fruit and rum.

Cut the dough in two. Roll out both pieces into rounds on a floured board, and use one round to line a tart tin. Spread in the filling. Dampen the edges of the pastry and lay on the second round. Press the edges together lightly with a fork. Cut a little hole in the top of the pie, brush the lid with milk and sprinkle with the granulated sugar.

Bake in the oven at 200°C (400°F) mark 6 for about 45 minutes until the pastry is crisp and brown. Transfer carefully to a wire rack to cool. The tart is lovely hot or cold. In Cumbria it is sometimes served with a dollop of rum butter.

Apple Pie

An apple pie – sharp-flavoured soft-cooked fruit hatted with a crisp buttery pastry – is the perfect complement to a fine joint of ham.

Serves 4–6

For the pastry
200 g (7 oz) plain flour
2.5 ml (½ tsp) salt
25 g (1 oz) caster sugar
50 g (2 oz) butter
50 g (2 oz) lard
30–45 ml (2–3 tbsp) ice-cold water

For the filling
900 g (2 lb) cooking apples
juice and grated zest of 1 lemon
50–100 g (2–4 oz) brown sugar
2–3 cloves

Make the pastry first. Sift the flour with the salt into a bowl and mix in the sugar. Cut the butter and the lard together into small pieces. Using your fingertips, rub the fat into the flour until the mixture looks like fine breadcrumbs. Using your hand like a spatula, work in enough cold water to give a soft but not sticky dough. The amount of water you need varies with the water content of the fat and dryness of the flour – use the minimum you need to give a rollable dough.

Leave the dough to rest under cover in a cool larder or the refrigerator for 30 minutes.

Make the filling: peel, quarter and core the apples. Cut the quarters into fine slices and toss with the lemon juice. Heap the apple slices with the sugar, lemon zest and cloves in a 20 cm (8 inch) pie dish – the filling should come up a bit over the top of the dish, or you can use a pie-funnel to hold up the crust. The amount of sugar depends on the sourness of the apples and your own personal taste. Pour in a little water to make juice.

Roll out the pastry on a floured board with a floured rolling pin to a size which will fit generously over the domed apples. Trim round the edge to give you a long ribbon of pastry for the double rim. Wet the edge of the dish and press the pastry ribbon all round. Pick up the pastry lid over the rolling pin and lay it gently over the filling, pressing it on to the dampened pastry ribbon round the edge. Crimp the edge with your finger to make a frill. Wet the top, prick it in a few places with a fork to let out the steam, and dredge with caster sugar.

Bake the pie in the oven at 200°C (400°F) mark 6 for 25–35 minutes until the pastry is golden and crisp.

Serve warm with whipped cream or a creamy egg custard.

Celebration Cooking

Elizabeth Ward's galley-style kitchen in her 16th-century stone farmhouse on the outskirts of Grewelthorpe in North Yorkshire is at the heart of her family's entertaining, and is usually crammed with people – all helping with the preparation and cooking.

'Naturally my idea of Christmas,' Elizabeth explains cheerfully, 'is *not* being in the kitchen – I'd rather spend time with everyone else, playing Monopoly.'

The secret of happy entertaining, she believes, is letting everyone do what they do best. And if you think that's a bit hazardous, you should know that the Wards are no strangers to dangerous sports. Elizabeth met her husband Trevor – one of the country's foremost hang-gliders – on the edge of a precipice.

'I take care of the shopping. People tend not to like shopping nowadays – they just whizz in and out of the supermarket. Round here, it's worth going to small local producers, though. We have a phenomenal game butcher, Beavers, at Masham, who sells lots of game when it's in season. I really like making stews with game – it's much better in liquid as the meat's naturally so dry. Venison is a lovely party dish, but for a meal for two, wild duck is gorgeous. Once you've eaten wild duck, you'll never want the farmed version again.

'Harrison's, a butcher in Ripon, has marvellous beef. And I make my own damson gin, and pickles and jellies – apple and redcurrant jellies, and tomato chutneys.

Cooking for large numbers always sounds daunting, but Elizabeth maintains it doesn't have to be. 'I think people try to do too much. If you have good ingredients, you don't have to fuss. I enjoy searching out good things. I love going to markets and bore everyone stiff with what I bring back. This year we holidayed in Provence. I picked up an idea to preserve our glut of greenhouse peaches in brandy, and brought back olives to make my very own tapenade.'

Yorkshire folk enjoy their food. The Wards grow most of their own herbs and vegetables, including potatoes, and are lucky enough to have a miller in the village and a beekeeper who sells honey. 'There's a winemaker down the road who produces delicious fruit wines,' Elizabeth adds, 'and in Harrogate a supplier of smoked Nidderdale trout, which I like to serve as a starter for special occasions'.

The menu which follows is suitable for any special occasion feast, including a Christmas dinner party.

Smoked Trout with Sesame Seed Buns

The trout needs minimum preparation and the buns can be quickly made with dried yeast. Elizabeth Ward uses a seed-enriched flour from Village Craft Flours, her local miller. Make up a double batch, and use half for a large round loaf to eat with cheese for supper – it will need about 40 minutes' baking.

Serves 8

4 smoked trout, skinned and roughly flaked

For the buns
700 g (1½ lb) wholemeal flour (with seeds, if possible)
50 g (2 oz) sesame seeds
50 g (2 oz) sunflower seeds
1 sachet quick-rise yeast

5 ml (1 tsp) salt
25 g (1 oz) lard, softened
450 ml (¾ pint) tepid water
milk or water for brushing

To serve
butter
black pepper
quartered lemons

First make up the bread dough for the buns, starting a couple of hours before you need it. Toss all the dry ingredients together, reserving a few seeds to sprinkle on top. Rub in the fat and work in the water to give a nice softish dough. Work it a little until it feels smooth. Set aside in its mixing bowl under a damp cloth to rise (or put in a turned-off oven with a tray of boiling water on the bottom).

When the dough has doubled in size – after 40–60 minutes – knock it down and knead well to distribute the air. Cut the dough into three pieces and work each into a little round bun. Arrange these on a greased baking sheet. Brush with milk or water and sprinkle with the reserved seeds. Set the buns to rise again until doubled in size –. for about 20 minutes in a warm kitchen. Bake in the oven at 220°C (425°F) mark 7 for 15–20 minutes or until the bases sound hollow when you tap them. Transfer to a wire rack to cool.

When the buns are cool, split them, spread with butter, then top with roughly flaked trout. Sprinkle with pepper and serve with lemon quarters.

Hedgehogged Honey-Roast Potatoes

This is a delicious way of cooking big potatoes. Elizabeth digs her own Wiljas and King Edwards, and brushes them with local honey for a party treat.

Serves 8

1.8 kg (4 lb) old potatoes, peeled	salt
100 g (4 oz) dripping	30–45 ml (2–3 tbsp) warmed honey

Make deep diagonal slashes in the potatoes in a cross-hatched design, rather as you would to the top of a farmhouse loaf, but much deeper.

Heat the dripping in a roasting tin, add the potatoes slashed-side up and salt them. Roast in the oven at 180°C (350°F) mark 4 – they will need 1–1½ hours, depending on size. Baste them regularly. The slashes should split open as they cook so they look like hedgehogs.

Paint the tops of the potatoes with honey 10 minutes before the end of the cooking time. If you do it any earlier, the honey will burn.

Red Cabbage with Apple

The bright colour of red cabbage will be preserved if you cook it lightly with apple.

Serves 8

1 small red cabbage, finely sliced	15 ml (1 tbsp) water
1 large Bramley apple, peeled, cored and sliced, or	
2 smaller eating apples, cubed	

Put all the ingredients in a saucepan. Cover and cook for 8–10 minutes, shaking the pan to stop it sticking, until the water has evaporated and the apples have softened into a sharp sauce. The cabbage should still be quite firm.

Little Yorkshire Puddings

Although Elizabeth is a Lancashire lass, she makes these to bulk out a meal whenever she has extra guests. She says that individual puddings made in tartlet tins are less temperamental and quicker to bake than a single large one. A 200 ml (7 fl oz) capacity teacup is used in this recipe.

Makes 12–18 small puddings

1 teacup plain flour	2.5 ml (½ tsp) salt
1 teacup milk	dripping
1 egg	

Whisk all the ingredients together, except for the dripping, until you have a smooth batter. Leave aside until everything is almost ready – although Elizabeth finds it doesn't make a scrap of difference if you let the batter rest or not.

Drop a nugget of dripping into each hole of a tartlet tin; choose one with nice deep holes. Put the tin in a preheated oven to get good and hot, then pour a dollop of batter into each hole, until it is two-thirds full.

Bake in the oven at 220°C (425°F) mark 7 for 7–8 minutes until the puddings are nicely puffed up and browned. Serve at once.

Venison with Blackberry Wine

Elizabeth marinates her venison in local dry blackberry wine (the winery is housed in an old cotton mill) to ensure that this lean meat remains juicy. She uses roe venison because the haunch is not too big, and includes any garden herbs that have survived into the winter.

Serves 6–8

2.3 kg (5 lb) haunch roe venison
150 ml (¼ pint) blackberry wine (or any dry fruit wine)
handful of mixed fresh herbs, chopped

salt and pepper
1 large knob beef dripping

To serve
redcurrant jelly

Put the joint in a casserole that will just accommodate it, and let it marinate for at least 3 hours with the wine and herbs. Season and dot with dripping. Cook, still in the marinade, loosely covered, in the oven at 180°C (350°F) mark 4 for 2 hours (i.e. 20 minutes for each 450 g (1 lb) plus 20 minutes for the pot). Turn and baste it regularly. Uncover 20 minutes before the end of the cooking time to brown the top.

Serve on hot plates, accompanied by the juices served in a gravy boat, and redcurrant jelly in a separate dish.

Brandied Fruit Filo Parcels

This is a variation on traditional mince pies. Use bought filo pastry to make a cluster of pretty little parcels of different shapes. Serve with thick yogurt.

Makes 24–30

1 large or 2 small packets filo pastry
melted butter

For the filling
100 g (4 oz) butter, melted
50 g (2 oz) dried figs, chopped
50 g (2 oz) dried pears, chopped
50 g (2 oz) sultanas
50 g (2 oz) raisins
50 g (2 oz) almonds, walnuts and hazelnuts, roughly chopped

1 apple, peeled, cored and grated
150 ml (¼ pint) brandy
juice of 1 orange

To finish
fine strips of orange zest
a few glacé cherries, cut into pieces
icing sugar to dust

To serve
Greek-style strained yogurt

Mix the filling ingredients together and moisten the grown-ups' share with brandy and the children's with orange juice. Let the dried fruit swell for a few hours. Drain out the excess moisture.

When working with filo, keep it wrapped in its cling-film or covered with a damp tea towel until the last moment; if not, the pastry dries out and splits.

To make the parcels, recruit people with neat fingers (children really like doing this as it allows plenty of scope for imaginative innovation). Allot different shapes of parcel to each filling so that you remember which are brandied.

To make crackers: lay out three sheets of filo pastry and brush between the layers with melted butter. Cut the sheet into four rectangles. Put a little dab of filling on the shorter edge of each rectangle. Roll up into a tiny bolster and pinch in the pastry at each end to form a cracker. Secure with a knot of orange zest and nick the ends to make a frill.

To make triangles: lay out and butter the filo as above, but cut the sheet into three long strips. Put a dab of filling one end, and fold over the first edge diagonally to make a triangle. Carry on folding diagonally over and over, first to one side then the other, until you have a neat little triangular parcel. Seal with a piece of glacé cherry securing a ribbon of orange zest.

To make scrolls: proceed as for the crackers, but tuck in the ends by folding the two long ends to overlap the line of filling a little, and then roll up like a cigar. Secure with a ribbon of orange zest.

To make purses: make these as for the crackers, cutting the buttered filo into four squares. Put a dab of filling in the middle of each square of pastry and pull up the corners like a handkerchief. Pinch together to enclose the filling, allowing the corners to fly loose. Tie the necks with a ribbon of orange zest.

Place all the little parcels on a buttered baking tray and brush with melted butter. Bake in the oven at 200°C (400°F) mark 6 for 8–10 minutes until nicely browned; they look prettiest if allowed to crisp and darken at the edges.

Dredge with icing sugar. These parcels are best served warm. Hand round a bowl of yogurt separately.

Keeping the Réveillon in Provence

If it hadn't been for Julius Caesar's spot of trouble with the Gauls, the British and the people of Provence might have shared the same Christmas traditions. For Roman Britain was once governed from Arles, the ancient capital of Provence.

While we are roasting the New World turkey and flaming the German pudding, Sylvette Jauffret, winemaker of the Domaine de Pont Royal near Aix-en-Provence, is keeping the *réveillon*, Christmas Eve celebration, with a fasting meal of garlic broth and salt cod. The meal doesn't end there, of course. After Midnight Mass comes the feast, with the roast partridges cooked with apples and chestnuts, followed by the traditional Thirteen Desserts.

No festival in Provence could possibly be celebrated without good wine, something that the Domaine has no shortage of. The Jauffret family home – which also houses the wine cellars – is a handsome 18th-century post-house set in 30 hectares of ochre-earthed vineyards.

As well as husband Jacques-Alfred and the couple's three children, the rest of the family come over from Aix – brothers, in-laws, cousins, every-one. 'We always have game, maybe a civet of hare, or wild boar if there are enough of us or the plump partridges I've watched helping themselves in my vineyards since spring.

'On Christmas Eve the *petit souper*, fasting supper, is served at eight. Then it's time for Mass. We do actually have Midnight Mass at midnight here – in some places it starts earlier. Then it's home at around 1.45 am to get the presents ready. Everyone puts their shoes round the tree to be filled – it's the only time I can get the children to clean their shoes properly,' Sylvette says. 'After that we carry on with the meal, the *gros souper*. It can be 3 am by the time we sit down, and dawn when we rise from the table.'

From then on, throughout the festival, the Thirteen Desserts are left out to be nibbled. Their components are fairly flexible, Sylvette says, but there are certain rules governing their arrangement. The nuts and raisins, representing the four begging orders of monks (*li pachichoi*) must be grouped together: almonds do duty for the barefoot Carmelites; hazelnuts for the brown habits of the Augustinians; black raisins for the Franciscans; dried figs for the grey-robed Dominicans. Then there must be prunes and dates (look for the double 0 formed by the two sides of the stone that denotes the Holy Infant's expression of delight at the taste); walnuts and mandarins. You can have oranges, but Sylvette prefers William pears, the stalk ends dipped in red sealing wax to keep them fresh. There must be black nougat and white; a 'Winter' melon – honeydew or Charentais; and black and white grapes, hung on a hook on the beam in the larder since harvest-time.

THE THIRTEEN DESSERTS

The full Thirteen Desserts comprise: Sweet Oil Bread (Pompe à L'Huile) (see page 173), Black Nougat and White Nougat (see page 172), hazelnuts, almonds, raisins, dried figs, prunes (or dried peaches), dates (Marseille imports these from Africa), walnuts, mandarin oranges (or quince paste), pears (or oranges), melon and black and white grapes.

Salt-Cod Purée

In the old days, salt cod was cheap and plentiful. This is no longer true. Choose it with care: it should be ivory white, but not too white or it will probably have been chemically bleached. If the backbone is still pink, it hasn't been in the salt for long enough. The middle cut is the best choice.

You need to start preparing this dish 24 hours in advance. I have used smoked haddock as a substitute: it's not authentic, but it tastes just as good.

Serves 6

450 g (1 lb) salt cod

To poach
1 medium onion, skinned and quartered
2 bay leaves
3 dried fennel twigs
1 strip of orange peel
5 peppercorns

For the brandade
1 potato, boiled and mashed, and still warm (optional, but it helps the emulsion)

2 garlic cloves, skinned and crushed
300 ml (1/2 pint) warm olive oil
30–45 ml (2–3 tbsp) warm cream
salt and pepper

To finish
black olives
toast triangles

Wash the salt cod and cut it into two to four pieces. Put it to soak overnight in a colander set in a large bowl of water. Change the water often, or leave the bowl under a trickle of running water.

Drain the cod. Put it in a saucepan with the quartered onion and the aromatics. Cover it with water and bring gently to the boil. Remove the cod as soon as the water gives a good belching sound, and throw in a glassful of cold water. Leave the cod for 5 minutes, drain and skin.

Pound the fish with the potato, the garlic and a little of the oil. Beat in the rest of the oil, adding the cream towards the end, until you have a thick purée. You can do this in a food processor.

Season the purée and divide it among six ramekins. Decorate with olives and serve warm with toast. It is very rich so each person needs only a little.

Garlic Broth

'*L'aigo boullido sauvo la vido* – garlic broth saves lives,' Sylvette says. It is a fine cure-all and mothers give it to their children when they are feeling ill.

Serves 6

12 garlic cloves, skinned and thinly
   sliced
1.1 litres (2 pints) water
60 ml (4 tbsp) olive oil
2–3 sage sprigs

5 ml (1 tsp) salt
100 g (4 oz) vermicelli
1 egg yolk

Simmer the garlic in the water and olive oil for 30 minutes. Five minutes before the end of the cooking time, slip in the sage: it turns the soup a pretty yellow colour. Add salt and vermicelli – it takes 2–3 minutes to cook. Take the broth off the heat and whisk a ladleful into the egg yolk. Stir the rest of the broth into the egg yolk and serve at once.

Stuffed Partridges with Apples

'My mother-in-law liked this,' Sylvette says. 'She came from Normandy where the food is all apples, soured cream and skate with black butter. Now I too buy apples by the crate and often de-glaze a sauce with soured cream.'

Serves 6

1 onion, skinned and chopped
30 ml (2 tbsp) butter or oil
100 g (4 oz) minced veal
100 g (4 oz) minced beef
900 g (2 lb) apples (Golden
   Delicious or reinettes)
450 g (1 lb) cooked, peeled
   chestnuts
5 ml (1 tsp) chopped fresh or dried
   thyme, plus extra for sprinkling

1 glass brandy or Armagnac
salt and pepper
1 egg
3 partridges, cleaned and singed
5–10 ml (1–2 tsp) vegetable oil

To finish
150 ml (¼ pint) soured cream or
   crème fraîche
50 g (2 oz) butter

Fry the onion in the butter or oil in a frying pan. Add the meat and cook gently until the meat is sealed. Peel and slice half the apples and add to the pan. Let them soften a little. Stir in half the chestnuts, squash them down slightly, then add the thyme. Sprinkle with brandy, cover and leave to stew gently for about 20 minutes, until the apples are quite mushy. Taste and season. Let the mixture cool, then work in the egg.

Stuff the partridges with the mixture. Tie their drumsticks with thread to keep them neat. Transfer them to a roasting tin. Trickle the oil over them and sprinkle with thyme, salt and pepper. Wrap any leftover stuffing in buttered foil and put it in the roasting tin with the partridges.

Roast in the oven at 200°C (400°F) mark 6 for the first 10 minutes. Then turn the oven down to 170°C (325°F) mark 3 and cook them for about 40 minutes so they make plenty of juice.

When the birds are cooked through and the drumsticks pull away from the body easily, either quarter or halve them. (No self-respecting French housewife would expect her husband, or anyone else for that matter, to carve at table.) Pile the stuffing on a warmed serving dish, and arrange the partridge pieces around it. De-glaze the pan juices with the soured cream. Season to taste.

Peel and quarter the rest of the apples and sauté in the butter, taking care that they do not lose their shape. Arrange them around the partridge joints. Warm the remaining chestnuts in the pan and sprinkle them over the stuffing. Moisten the birds with a little of the sauce, and serve the rest separately.

Apple and Walnut Tart

Apples are the fruit of the Provençal winter – and reinettes are the classic Provençal apple. Golden Delicious and Granny Smiths are also popular. French apple tarts are never sharp.

Serves 6–8

For the rich shortcrust pastry
175 g (6 oz) unsalted butter
200 g (7 oz) plain flour
22.5 ml (1½ tbsp) icing sugar
a little ice cold water

For the filling
225 g (8 oz) walnuts
900 g (2 lb) yellow apples
45 ml (3 tbsp) honey
1 small egg yolk for glazing

Make the pastry: rub the butter into the flour. Sprinkle in the sugar and the minimum amount of water needed to make a workable dough. It should have a dry, firm consistency. Leave under cover in a cool place for at least 30 minutes until hard.

Reserve a quarter for the lattice-work, then roll out the rest thinly, and use it to line a 30 cm (12 inch) tin. Reserve about 12 of the walnuts and grind the rest to a powder in a food processor.

Peel and core the apples: slice them finely vertically. Sprinkle the powdered walnuts over the pastry. Arrange the apple slices in concentric circles until all the pastry is hidden, then pour the honey over.

Roll out the reserved pastry and cut into strips. Lay a pastry lattice over the apples, and dot the interstices with reserved walnuts. Glaze the lattice and the edges of the tart with egg yolk. Bake in the oven at 180°C (350°F) mark 4 for about 40–45 minutes. Serve warm.

White Nougat

Most household nougat recipes involve a lot of tricky work with a sugar thermometer. But this is an easy version from Georges de Mauduit's *The Vicomte in the Kitchen* (1933).

Makes about 450 g (1 lb)

100 g (4 oz) blanched almonds	2 egg whites
25 g (1 oz) shelled pistachio nuts	1–2 drops vanilla essence
350 g (12 oz) icing sugar	2 sheets of rice paper

Cut the nuts into strips and mix them with the icing sugar. Work in the egg whites and vanilla essence. Beat with a wooden spoon until you have a smooth paste. Spread the mixture on a sheet of rice paper laid on a baking sheet. It should be about the thickness of a finger. Lay the other sheet of rice paper over the top and cover with a baking sheet, lightly weighted.

Leave it to dry out in a warm place – it will be ready in about a week. Cut into ribbons.

Black Nougat

This recipe for *Le nougat noir de Mireille* is from Sylvette's favourite Christmas book, *Misé Lipeto: Le Calendrier Gourmand de la Cuisine Provençale d'hier et d'aujourd'hui.*

Makes about 700 g (1½ lb)

1 small knob of butter	225 g (8 oz) unskinned almonds
450 g (1 lb) set honey	2 sheets of rice paper

You need either a tin mould or a wooden frame, 25 x 15 x 2.5 cm (10 x 6 x 1 inches) with detachable sides. Butter the mould, if you are using one, and cool it in the refrigerator.

Pour the honey into a small saucepan and heat it gently for 5–6 minutes until it melts and comes to the boil. Remove from the heat and stir in the almonds. Put it back on the heat. It will come back to the boil in 8–9 minutes, and froth up. Cook it gently for another 30–35 minutes, stirring all the time and taking care that the almonds are kept away from the sides. The nougat is ready when a drop of the syrup makes a firm ball when dropped in cold water.

At this point, take the pan off the heat and continue to stir the mixture for another 10 minutes or so, until it cools. Line the mould or frame with rice paper: if using a frame, set it on a marble slab. Pour in the cooled mixture.

Top the mixture with the other sheet of rice paper. Set a board on top to weight it and leave for 30 minutes to set – no longer, or you'll never get it unstuck. Keep in a cool place as this nougat has a tendency to melt, unlike the commercially prepared variety. Cut it into pieces with kitchen scissors, or break it with a knife tapped with a hammer.

Sweet Oil Bread

This bread, which represents Jesus, is much richer than everyday bread. It should be broken, never cut with a knife.

Makes 2 loaves

900 g (2 lb) strong bread flour
75 g (3 oz) fresh yeast
300 ml (¹/₂ pint) warm water
225 g (8 oz) caster sugar
15 ml (1 tbsp) aniseeds (optional)

scant 300 ml (¹/₂ pint) olive oil
15 ml (1 tbsp) orange flower water
sweet black coffee or an egg yolk
 for glazing

Sift the flour into a large warm bowl. Mix the yeast in a small bowl with half a glass of the warm water. Stir in 5 heaped tablespoons of the flour – enough to work into a dough ball. Cut a deep cross in the ball and put it in a bowl of warm water until it swells and bobs to the surface.

Mix the caster sugar and aniseeds, if using, into the warm flour. Make a well in the centre. Pour in the oil and drop in the ball of wet yeast dough, the orange flower water and a little more warm water. Work all well together, adding extra water until you have a soft dough. Cut the dough in two and knead each half into a ball.

Oil two large baking sheets and dust them lightly with flour. Roll each ball into a flat round on a well-floured board. Transfer these to the baking sheets and pat them out evenly with your hand until they are about 30 cm (12 inches) across. Put to rise in a warm, draught-free place under a clean cloth for 5–7 hours. Preheat the oven to 150°C (300°F) mark 2 and place a roasting pan of boiling water on the bottom. Brush the breads with coffee or egg yolk and bake for 10 minutes, then raise the heat to 200°C (400°F) mark 6. Bake for another 20 minutes until well risen and brown.

TRUFFLING IN PROVENCE

There's nothing like the scent of a fresh truffle just dug from the damp stony earth in a patch of scrub oak in Provence. The perfume is so rich and heady it warms the icy winter air with that inimitable sensuous odour – strong enough, the French writer Colette explains, for a basket of new-laid eggs to absorb the flavour through their shells. Truffle-scented eggs, scrambled or as an omelette, were her favourite dish.

There's magic in finding the black diamonds, too – in the secret search for buried treasure. There is also a particular excitement in the very ordinariness of both the landscape and the participants, who are mostly peasant farmers with the patience to wait the 25 years it takes for the truffle's host-tree to mature into productivity.

Here in these wintry woods, at any time from late November to early March, are to be found no scarlet-clad horsemen and baying hounds – just the battered boot of an old *camionnette* protruding from a scrawny tangle of undergrowth, and the dun-clad treasure-seeker, with a small pickaxe and scruffy little dog, quartering the stony, barren-looking ground in between a few lines of scrubby kermes oak.

Truffle hunters are a solitary race – solitary apart from their hounds. The dogs have no special breeding, but they come from a particular line – mongrels which, nevertheless, have a real market value of roughly their own weight in the black diamonds they nose out.

The dog is not naturally interested in the black tuber, that is the pig's forte, except that a pig cannot be trained not to gobble what he grubs up. The dog has to be trained to pick out the perfume, which becomes richer as the truffle matures.

A human can nose out truffles, too – old spinsters with little on their mind are said to be the best – and there are sometimes a few indicators to help: a crack in the soil near a host tree and a cloud of tiny reddish flies. But a good dog will find ten times as many.

'You must treat a dog well,' the truffle hunter told me. 'He needs a lot of love and encouragement. He must be quarantined the night before the course, and go without his supper and his breakfast. You call off the dog as soon as he finds the truffle – don't let him scrape too long or he hurts his paws and won't work.'

Each owner has his own method of training. Some start with a bit of truffled omelette to give the hound a taste for the job. Then the proud owner shows a real truffle to his dog, buries it in a patch of ground and rewards him when he finds it. After that the reward is a bit of bread, scented with the truffle the dog has just found.

The truffle market is a very discreet affair. The casual passer-by would not even know it was happening. The truffle men, and a few women, gather in loose knots at the rendezvous – maybe in a corner of the market square, or near a café accessible to the main road, so that the buyers, the men-from-Paris, can slip in and out in their diesel Moroodoo without leaving a ripple on the surface of the town. No one talks – it is enough to nod and exchange brief greetings. Anything more might affect the as yet unfixed price.

A few large saloon cars arrive. Suddenly trestle tables are set up and the bags come out. Although most of the truffles are small, some are as big as a fist, and occasionally one – the stuff of legends – is the size of a small football. The men-from-Paris examine the crop. Smell first, then look, then touch. Deals are done. It's over. The bar fills with the mingled scents of truffle, pastis and *café-crème*. The men-from-Paris slide away.

A Traditional Irish Christmas

The whole point of an Irish Christmas is that there must be a gathering of family and friends. The more the merrier: Irish families no longer run to a rugby team, but they can still field more than most.

A blazing log fire holds the winter at bay, even though the beautiful hills of Munster can never be really unkind to man or beast. This is not the wild rocky hilliness of the west coast, but the gentle landscape of the east – green and soft, with rich pastures for the dairy herds that have long supplied the traders of Cork with the wherewithal to provision the world's ships. Every time the English went to war the merchant princes of Cork rebuilt their mansions. The Duke of Wellington stocked up in Cork – salt beef and salt pork put up in barrels. The pickling trade left a lot of offal going begging and, in the early 18th century, the cellarmen, who had charge of the casks for the salt meat, were paid 7 lb of offal a day in addition to their usual wages.

Offal and salt meat are now the speciality of Cork's English Market – named after the traders who, in the old days, controlled it. The inhabitants of Cork still consume four times the national average of offal – 20 lb a year per head – and there's always a queue at the tripe and *drisheen* stall. Drisheen is an unseasoned blood-only black pudding. In the Christmas run-up, the market stalls are piled high with spiced beef, a vital part of any Irish Christmas, and the cold air is heavy with the powdery fragrance of Jamaica pepper, cloves and cinnamon.

Other ingredients are essential in order to achieve a proper 'crack' (the word the Irish use to describe a really good time). No gathering is complete without fistfuls of the local brew, a good group of storytellers and maybe a bit of singing. Some of the finest tales to be heard in Ireland are told by Declan Ryan, chef-proprietor of Cork's Arbutus Lodge and heir to the

Atlantic provisioners, in the company of his old friend the potter Stephen Pearce and his wife Kim Mai Mooney and a congenial gathering of family and friends. Among them are Myrtle and Ivan Allen from Ballymaloe, round the bay from Stephen's pottery. They run their celebrated hotel as a family business, although their daughter-in-law Darina also has a television series and cookery books to her credit.

Everyone lends a hand in the preparation of Christmas dinner, which has to be on the table no later than 5.30 pm, to allow time for the singing afterwards.

After the meal, everyone settles down to the real business of the evening, making music and telling tales. Such an evening, candlelit, in the company of old friends, leads to the inevitable hangover. The Cork cure for that is a dish of *crubeens* – pig's trotters. Declan is a firm advocate of the remedy. Come St Stephen's Day – Boxing Day – this year, he surely won't be the only one putting its efficacy to the test.

Mixed Ballygowan Seafood

Local fisherman John Tattan often brings in mussels and Dublin Bay prawns. Freshly and simply prepared, this dish keeps fingers busy and hunger away while the goose is cooking.

Serves 6–8

1 glass white wine
2–3 shallots or 1 small onion, skinned and chopped
30 ml (2 tbsp) chopped fresh parsley

1.8 kg (4 lb/4 pints) well-scrubbed mussels
700 g (1½ lb) Dublin Bay prawns
lemon wedges
salt

Bring the white wine, shallots and parsley to the boil in a large flat pan with a lid (a wok is perfect). Throw the mussels into this broth, cover the pan and leave them to open for 5–8 minutes.

While the mussels are cooking, drop the prawns into plenty of salted boiling water. Drain the prawns as soon as they come back to the boil.

Serve the mussels with their broth in a big dish. The prawns are nicest when they have just cooled: serve them in a separate dish. Accompany with lemon wedges and salt.

Carrot Curls

The damp peaty soil of Ireland seems to produce huge succulent root vegetables. At this time of year carrots are particularly fine. They are easiest to scrape when they still have the damp earth on them.

Serves 6–8

900 g (2 lb) long fat carrots
50 g (2 oz) butter

salt and pepper

Scrape the carrots clean. With a potato peeler, cut long thin curls down the full length of each vegetable: only peel the outside dark orange flesh (use the inside for a stock or stew).

Steam the carrots strips briefly, so they retain the curl. Meanwhile, melt the butter and season with salt and pepper. Pile the carrots into a dish and pour the melted butter over them before serving.

Honeyed Sea-Beet

Sea-beet, with its firm, spinach-like leaves, grows wild along the coast of Ireland. Kim Mai loves its crisp salty flavour, but says gathering it is hazardous: she nearly drowned in a peat bog one time she went collecting.

Serves 6–8

900 kg (2 lb) sea-beet, perpetual spinach or Swiss chard leaves	2 garlic cloves, skinned and finely chopped
50 g (2 oz) butter	30 ml (2 tbsp) honey

Strip the sea-beet leaves from the stalks. Shred the leaves roughly, rinse them thoroughly, and then parboil them briefly in the water still clinging to them. Meanwhile, melt the butter with the garlic and honey in a small saucepan. Drain the sea-beet, pressing out all the water, and then turn the leaves in the butter mixture.

Braised Jerusalem Artichokes

Serves 6–8

900 g (2 lb) Jerusalem artichokes
50 g (2 oz) butter
30 ml (2 tbsp) runny honey
30–45 ml (2–3 tbsp) water
salt and pepper

To finish
honey
extra butter

Peel the artichokes and cut into similar sizes. Arrange in a single layer in a gratin dish, dot with butter, sprinkle with honey and water; season.

Cover with foil and cook in the oven at 130°C (250°F) mark 1 for 1 hour or so. If the oven is full, they can stew gently on a very low top heat, and will need less time – shake the pan occasionally (add extra water when necessary).

When tender, add another splash of honey and butter, and turn up the heat to caramelise the outsides. Add a splash of water to dilute the juices and give a shiny caramel coating.

Roast Goose with Champ Stuffing

Serves 6–8

For the goose
3.6–5.6 kg (8–12 lb) goose
salt and pepper
1.8 kg (4 lb) potatoes
450 g (1 lb) leeks, trimmed and
    sliced finely
50 g (2 oz) butter

For the apples
8 apples, washed and cored
60 ml (4 tbsp) sultanas and raisins
100 g (4 oz) brown sugar, honey or
    treacle
50 g (2 oz) butter
8 cloves

Wipe the goose, singe off any stray feathers and fine hairs, and season it inside and out.

Make the champ stuffing: scrub the potatoes and cook them in salted water. When soft, drain them, dry them off and shake them over the heat so that they split to show their floury insides. Discard the peel and mash the potatoes.

Turn the leeks in the butter, along with the water that clings to the leeks after washing. Shake them over the heat until they wilt. Beat the leeks and their juices into the mash. Taste and season as necessary. Stuff the goose with the hot champ. Sew up the opening.

Roast the goose in the oven at 180°C (350°F) mark 4 on a rack over a baking tray full of water for 15 minutes per 450 g (1 lb) (the stuffing is already fully cooked and hot, so you do not need to include it in the weight calculations). In the beginning, pour out the goose fat as it runs into the tray. You will have to keep replacing the water.

Arrange the apples on a baking sheet, and stuff each cavity with the dried fruit and sugar, honey or treacle. Finish each with a dot of butter and a clove. Bake in the bottom of the goose-oven for 1 hour, or until soft.

Pierce the goose's thigh to test if it's done: the juices should run clear. Let the bird sit for 15 minutes or so, then carve it in long slices parallel to the breast-bone and serve a baked apple and a little champ with each portion.

Spice-Crusted Salt Beef

Spiced beef is one of the spin-offs from Cork's historic victualling trade, and can be found on sale in the city's English Market. This is a favourite Christmas cut-and-come-again dish throughout Ireland, but only in Cork is it enjoyed all year round.

Serves about 12

1.8 kg (4 lb) joint salt beef (buy a piece that has been in the brine for only 3–4 days)

For the crust
175 g (6 oz) ground allspice
50 g (2 oz) ground cinnamon
25 g (1 oz) ground cloves

Dry the meat thoroughly. Mix the spices and rub them all over the beef. Set the meat on a bed of the spices in a bowl and heap the remaining spices around and over it to make an airtight crust.

Leave in a cool place for at least a week, turning the beef every now and again and piling back the spices. If it weeps a little brine, just mop it up and dust it dry with spices. The longer the beef is left in the spices, the longer it will last.

When you are ready to cook it, shake off loose spices (they are lovely in stews and gravies) and transfer the joint, without disturbing the spice crust, into a saucepan with enough cold water to submerge it. Simmer for 2–3 hours until it is tender. Drain the joint – there should still be a nice spice crust on it, and press it under a weight overnight. You can keep it in the refrigerator for 3–4 weeks. Serve it cut into thin slices, with a fresh salad and potatoes boiled Irish-style in their jackets, or in sandwiches with chutney.

Brown Soda Bread

'To me this says Ireland,' says Declan. 'If anyone asked me what is the most Irish of all things, I would say soda bread. Brown was the usual – white would only be for very special occasions: if people included butter they would call it cake. It used to be baked in a bastable – a heavy iron pot with three legs and a reversible lid for the peat coals. If it's cooked in that, it will have a slightly built-up edge where the dough meets the side of the pot. A friend of my mother's used to put her bastable in the oven when she had one installed.'

Makes 1 large loaf

450 g (1 lb) brown stoneground flour	**2.5 ml (½ tsp) salt**
175 g (6 oz) white flour	**50 g (2 oz) butter (optional)**
2.5 ml (½ tsp) baking soda	**buttermilk or soured cream**
	1 small egg

Mix all the dry ingredients together. If using the butter, mix it in with your fingertips.

Work in the buttermilk and the egg. The mixture must be really wet so that it only just holds its shape.

Place it on a greased, floured baking tray and shake it to settle it flat. Cut a deep cross very firmly into the top. Bake in the oven at 200°C (400°F) mark 6 for 40 minutes until firm and browned.

White Christmas Cake

This is Darina Allen's recipe: it makes a change from the usual heavy Christmas cake. The basic mix is an angel cake, and only the palest dried fruit and candied peel are used. It is finished with toasted marzipan, cutting out some of the work since it does not need to be iced with white frosting later. Make this cake no more than a week before Christmas, as it does not improve with keeping.

Makes 1 cake

150 g (5 oz) butter
200 g (7 oz) plain flour
pinch of salt
1.25 ml (1/4 tsp) baking powder
5 ml (1 tsp) lemon juice
5 ml (1 tsp) Irish whiskey
75 g (3 oz) ground almonds
6 egg whites
225 g (8 oz) caster sugar
50 g (2 oz) finely chopped candied
   peel (preferably home-made)
75–100 g (3–4 oz) green or yellow
   cherries, halved

For the almond paste
about 225 g (8 oz) ground almonds
225 g (8 oz) caster sugar
1 egg
a drop of almond essence
30 ml (2 tbsp) Irish whiskey
icing sugar for dusting

To finish
1 egg, separated

Line a 17.5 cm (7 inch) diameter, 7.5 cm (3 inch) deep, cake tin with greaseproof paper. Cream the butter until very soft. Sift in the flour, salt and baking powder, then add the lemon juice, whiskey and ground almonds.

Whisk the egg whites until quite stiff, add the caster sugar gradually and whisk again until stiff and smooth. Stir some of the egg white into the butter mixture and then carefully fold in the rest. Lastly, add the chopped peel and the halved cherries.

Pour into the prepared tin and bake in the oven at 170°C (325°F) mark 3 for about 1 1/2 hours until firm to the touch. Allow the cake to cool a little, then transfer it to a wire rack. Finish it the following day.

Next day, make the almond paste. Mix the almonds and the sugar. Beat the egg with the almond essence and the whiskey and work it into the dry ingredients (you may need extra ground almonds). Sprinkle the worktop with icing sugar, turn out the almond paste and work it lightly until smooth.

Put a sheet of greaseproof paper on to the worktop; dust with some icing sugar. Take about half the almond paste and roll it out on the paper until you have a circle large enough to cover the top of the cake. Paint the top of the cake with lightly beaten egg white, and put the cake, sticky side down, on to the almond paste. Give the cake a thump to make sure the paste sticks, and then cut round the edge. Keep the extra bits to make hearts or holly leaves.

Measure the circumference of the cake with a piece of string. Roll out two strips of almond paste to half this length on greaseproof paper; trim both to the height of the cake. Paint both the cake and almond paste with egg white. Press the strips against the sides of the cake so all the edges meet, and peel off the paper. Use a straight-sided glass to even the edges.

Roll out the trimmings and cut out hearts or holly or whatever you please. Paint the cake all over with egg yolk and stick on the hearts. Paint the hearts with egg yolk. Let the cake dry a little then lift it on to a baking tray. Bake in the oven at 220°C (425°F) mark 7 for 15–20 minutes until slightly toasted.

NEW YEAR

As the old year is buried, the new year is born. It's time to look forward to the future. At this time of year, traditional celebrations reflect our uncertainty about what lies ahead for all of us. We feast at New Year as a sacrifice to unpredictable gods, offering promises to do better in the coming months.

Disentangling the festival of Christmas from New Year is an almost impossible task. The one is as Christian as the church can make it, the other still owes allegiance to more unruly predecessors, but the two remain completely intertwined. Such celebrations are preoccupied with universal concerns: death and birth, and the hope that maybe the phoenix of spring will rise from the ashes of winter.

Among rural communities, each takes care of his own. Herdsmen and shepherds look forward to the time when their animals drop their young, and spring pastures can be cropped again. Those who work the land prepare for the spring sowing as the danger of frost recedes.

Inshore fishermen wait for the winter storms to subside and, in the far north, watch for the reopening of harbours closed by ice. In the old days at this time, coastal dwellers could feast in safety in the certainty that invaders would not brave the frozen oceans – an added bonus for an island nation such as Britain where few of the villages were more than a couple of days' march from the sea.

So, in these islands, there's nowhere where the mind is more concentrated on the turning year than in Scotland, always vulnerable to invasion from the north, where Hogmanay is celebrated with the pipes, a ceilidh and a riotous feast. The custom of first-footing ensures that the first visitor over the doorstep is friend and not foe. When a blond-haired stranger was likely to be a marauding Viking, a dark-haired firstfooter is naturally the most welcome. The visitor best confirms his friendly intentions with a skirl of the pipes and a bit of fuel to stoke the fire. The reward is a dram of whisky and a piece of something nice – maybe cloutie dumpling, gingerbread or a slice of the baker's deliciously rich Black Bun.

National aspirations surface in New Year customs. The Germans, preoccupied with prosperity, serve carp with a sweet spicy sauce, and save a round shiny scale from the fish to be tucked away in the purse to ensure good business in the year to come.

The Italians have a dish of stuffed pork-trotters and lentils – the little seeds offering a promise of future fertility.

In southern Spain we used to put up the last of the year's grapes in anise-flavoured brandy, and ate one for each stroke of midnight – a feat which left everyone dizzy but guaranteed well-loaded vines for the following year.

I remember too, when we lived in Provence, that the French seemed more concerned with romance, marking the turning year with aphro-disiac oysters and champagne.

However we choose to celebrate, the cycle of the year is now complete. It is a symbol of hope for the future that the loaded table reflects the plentiful harvest of summer, the prudent husbandry of autumn.

So, at the end of the New Year feast – just as the clock strikes midnight – go out and look in the nettle patch at the end of the garden. Who knows? Tucked away under the dead brown leaves of winter, you may find the first green shoots of spring.

Recipe Listings

Index

Addresses

Spring in Herefordshire:
Hope End Hotel,
Hope End,
Ledbury,
Herefordshire
HR8 1JQ
(01531-633613)

Food from the Sea:
Network Fisheries Ltd,
West Quay,
Newhaven,
East Sussex
(01273-513 884)

Spring in the Garden of
England:
Cooper and Son,
Roman Road,
Aldington,
Near Ashford,
Kent TN25 7DH
(01233-720231)

A Mail-order Feast:
Heal Farm,
Kings Nympton,
Umberleigh,
Devon
EX37 9TB
(017695-74341)

Loch-side Cooking:
Tiroran House,
Isle of Mull,
Argyll PA69 6ES
(016815-232)

Take Two Norfolk
Cooks:
Humble Pie,
Market Place,
Burnham Market,
King's Lynn,
Norfolk PE31 8HE
(01328-738581)

Summer in Ireland:
Glassdrumman Lodge,
85 Mill Road,
Annalong,
Co. Down BT34 4RH
Northern Ireland
(03967-68585)

Apple Harvest:
Ivor and Susie Dunkerton,
Hays Head,
Luntley, Pembridge,
Leominster,
Herefordshire HR6 9ED
(015447-653)

Mrs Sarah Sage and Mrs
Charis Ward,
Abbey Dore Court Garden,
Near Hereford HR2 0AD
(01981-240279)

Winter Breakfasts:
The Creggans Inn,
Strachur,
Argyll PA27 8BX
(0136986-279)

A Traditional Irish
Christmas:
Ballymaloe Country
House & Restaurant,
Shanagarry,
Midleton,
County Cork
(010-353-21 652531)

Arbutus Lodge Hotel,
Montenotte,
Cork City,
County Cork
(010-353-21 501237)

You may be interested in other titles in the series, also published by Ebury Press:

The Essential Mosimann   *Anton Mosimann*   £9.99

Food for Friends   *Sophie Grigson*   £9.99

Roast Chicken & Other Stories   *Simon Hopkinson*   £10.99

Wild Food from Land and Sea   *Marco Pierre White*   £9.99

Available from good bookshops or telephone Murlyn Services on 01279 427203.
You may pay by cheque/postal order/credit card and should allow 28 days for
delivery. Postage and packing are free.